St. Louis Community
College

Library

5801 Wilson Avenue
St. Louis, Missouri 63110

Two Thousand Years of

ORIENTAL CERAMICS

Two Thousand Years of
ORIENTAL CERAMICS

FUJIO KOYAMA

A N D

JOHN FIGGESS

HARRY N. ABRAMS, INC.

Publishers, New York

Library of Congress Catalog Card Number 60-10344
No part of the contents of this book may be reproduced
without the written permission of the publishers
HARRY N. ABRAMS, INC., NEW YORK, N. Y.
Produced by Bijutsu Shuppan-Sha, Tokyo
Printed and bound in Japan

TABLE OF CONTENTS

INTRODUCTION

EARTHENWARE pots for use as water jars, cooking vessels, food utensils, grain storage containers, and so on have been fashioned by men all over the world from the earliest times; but it was in the area of the Far East more than two thousand years ago that the manufacture of pottery departed from the purely utilitarian sphere and, developing in a spectacular manner, ultimately became a great art. The countries of this region, comprising China, Annam, Thailand, Korea, and Japan, all participated to a greater or lesser extent in the movement, but the foremost was China, where a high-fired and technically well-developed type of glazed pottery—the forerunner of the famous celadon wares of later eras—was being made at least as early as the Han period (206 B.C.–220 A.D.). By the fourth or fifth century the Chinese potters were producing porcelaneous stonewares with hard vitreous glazes in black and various shades of green color fused at a high temperature to form part of the body—something quite unknown in the world up to that time. By the end of the eleventh century, that is, before the flight of the Sung Court to the south in the face of the invading Chin Tartars, the technique of ceramic manufacture in China had progressed to the highest point ever reached in its history, and hundreds of kilns all over the country were turning out glazed stonewares and porcelain of unsurpassed excellence in an unparalleled range of designs, forms, and colors. Chinese influence and ceramic techniques also flowed at this time into the neighboring countries and especially into Korea and Annam, where pottery manufacture flourished, with the result that from the tenth to the thirteenth centuries high-class ceramic wares were produced in large quantities throughout the region of the Far East.

European interest in Chinese pottery and porcelain was first aroused through the medium of export wares which reached the Islamic countries of the Near and Middle East after the Mongol conquest, and which were imported in quite large quantities during the fourteenth and fifteenth centuries. Kings, princes, and peers of European nations began eagerly to collect the prized porcelain wares, which led to serious efforts being applied to making porcelain in Europe. The first man to succeed in this was a German, Johann Friedrich Böttger of Dresden, who, after repeated failures, successfully fired the first European-made porcelain wares early in the eighteenth century. The manufacture of true porcelain in Europe thus came at least a thousand years after it was first made in the Far East.

Of all the famous pottery-producing countries in the Far East, Japan was perhaps the slowest in developing a full-fledged ceramic industry, no doubt because of the traditional Japanese reliance on lacquer ware rather than pottery for everyday use; but after the opening

[7]

of the country to the West in the middle of the nineteenth century, Japanese pottery and porcelain manufacture forged ahead rapidly, and today Japan is perhaps the foremost producer in the world.

The study of the development of pottery in the Far East, a subject about which surprisingly little was known previous to the end of the nineteenth century, has made good progress in the last fifty years, thanks to the excavation of a number of old kiln sites and tombs and the investigations of European and American scholars, as well as the efforts of Chinese and Japanese research workers. But our knowledge is still only fragmentary, and much which remains obscure can be cleared up only by continuing patient research. Some things perhaps will never be known.

Unfortunately, since the end of the Second World War it has been impossible for Japanese to carry out first-hand investigations at kiln sites on the continent of Asia, and original research by Japanese scholars on Chinese and Korean ceramics is thereby seriously hampered, but we have endeavored in this book to present a short survey in outline of the development of Oriental ceramics, based mainly on the data assembled before the war, supplemented by the published results of more recent research carried out by Chinese scholars.

Fujio Koyama
John Figgess

AN OUTLINE HISTORY OF CHINESE CERAMICS FROM ANCIENT TIMES TO THE T'ANG PERIOD

THE manufacture of pottery in China is of very remote origin, and although researches of the last fifty years have thrown much light on the subject, a great area still remains obscure. Until fairly recently it was thought that the art of glazing pottery was not developed in China until the Han period (206 B.C.–220 A.D.) but it is now fairly well established that it was practiced at least as early as the Western Chou period (1050–770 B.C.), and there is some evidence that glazed wares were made in the Shang-Yin period (1766–1050 B.C.), although it is not yet decided whether the glaze on Yin pottery was artificially applied or merely the natural result of wood ash falling on the pottery during firing. In the Nelson Gallery of Art in Kansas City, there is a low-fired, green-glazed pottery jar of a bronze-type shape unmistakably attributable to the Warring States period, which demonstrates that at this time the art of glazing was known to the Chinese potter. Chinese ceramic technique was, however, only in an embryonic stage of development during the Han and Six Dynasties (222–589 A.D.) periods, and, as compared with the following T'ang (618–906 A.D.) and Sung (960–1279) periods, kilns were few and pottery technique was at a relatively low level. Nevertheless, some of the wares datable to this period have a kind of placid charm and primitive strength not found in products of later times, and in recent years these pieces have come to be admired by connoisseurs of Chinese ceramics throughout the world.

The glazes used from the Warring States to the Han and Six Dynasties periods may be divided broadly into two categories: those containing lead or soda which fuse at a temperature of about 800 to 900 degrees centigrade; and ash glazes and feldspathic glazes, which require a temperature of 1200 to 1300 degrees for complete fusion. These two techniques, which are known respectively as "low-fired" or "soft-fired" glaze, and "high-fired" or "hard-fired" glaze, have been employed in China for more than two thousand years and are still in use today. Low-fired glazes were possibly introduced into China from the West through Central Asia, but the high-fired glaze is a Chinese invention. The earliest known type of pottery with a high-fired feldspathic glaze is the brownish-green celadon ware which seems to have been manufactured at a number of places in the provinces of Chekiang and Fukien from about the middle of the Han period. This ware, which is commonly called Yüeh ware, seems to have been originated during the Han dynasty and was evidently turned out in large quantities and in a wide variety of shapes throughout the period of the Six Dynasties and in T'ang times. Some of the kilns which produced Yüeh have been discovered. Particularly worthy of note are the Chiu-yen or "Nine Rocks" kiln located about five miles northwest of Shaohsing hsien in Chekiang which was first discovered by Mr. Yuzo Matsumura in 1936 and subsequently visited by the English scholar Brankston, and the Tê-ch'ing kiln at Tê-ch'ing hsien, also in Chekiang, discovered by Mr. Yasuo Yanaiyama in 1930. A third kiln site which yielded shards of Yüeh type was reported at Nan-tai near Fu-chou in Fukien province, and this was visited by Professor Plumer of the University of Michigan in 1935.

Celadon wares of the Tê-ch'ing, Nan-tai, and Chiu-yen kilns bear so close a resemblance to one another that it is not always easy to distinguish between them, but a close examination reveals slight differences of body, glaze, form, and technique. The most plentiful of the surviving wares are those of the Chiu-yen kiln, and a large quantity of these were taken to Japan in the thirties (plate 1). Some time in 1936, during the construction of a military road between Hangchow and Ningpo, a group of ancient tombs was discovered near Shaohsing, and excavation of this site led to the discovery of a large quantity of celadon wares attributable to the Chiu-yen kiln of Yüeh Chou, together with a considerable number of bronze articles. This news spread abroad and led to unauthorized digging and looting of the ancient tombs in the area, with the result that the antique markets were suddenly flooded with a great number of Yüeh celadon wares. According to report, more than three thousand ancient tombs were discovered in two areas near the city of Nan ch'ih, two and one-half miles south of Shaohsing, and in the neighborhood of Ko ch'iao ch'en, seven and one-half miles to the northwest. In some of these tombs, mortuary records of the T'ang and Sui (589-618 A.D.) dynasties were found, but the greater number evidently were of earlier date, as a number of bronze mirrors and a few celadon pots inscribed with dates of manufacture testified. The great majority of the Yüeh wares excavated from these ancient tombs were of the Chiu-yen type, including large pots, jars with four ears, plates, bowls, ewers, tripod vessels, candlestands, and wine cups, and all were evidently made as tomb ornaments.

Of the Nan-tai type of Yüeh ware only very few pieces are known; and there are a few celadon wares apparently of Six Dynasties provenance which cannot be identified with known products of any of the three kilns mentioned above. During the Six Dynasties period the Yüeh kilns also produced a variety of attractive pottery covered with an intense black high-fired glaze (plate 17). In 1932 Mr. Yasuo Yonaiyama discovered a number of fragments of ware of this kind (which the Japanese call *temmoku*) together with some celadon shards at a Six Dynasties kiln site near Tê-ch'ing in Chekiang, and in 1955 Chinese Government archaeologists excavating tomb sites of the Six Dynasties period near Nanking unearthed a number of ewers, among them at least two with opaque black glaze. One of these came from a tomb which can be reliably dated to the fifth century A.D.

According to ancient Chinese literary references, the ceramics produced in the Six Dynasties period included, besides celadon and *temmoku* wares, a white glazed pottery. No kiln site has yet been discovered for such pottery, although it is generally believed that there was a kiln near the village of Pai yao at the foot of Mount Pi-chia in Kwangtung which made white ware in ancient times. It is also conjectured that the famous pottery center of Ching-tê-chên was already operating during the Six Dynasties, and, although no firm evidence exists to show that white wares were made there at that time, occasionally shards of white pottery are seen which have definite characteristics of the Six Dynasties period and which could conceivably have been made at Ching-tê-chên.

During the Han period, and for several centuries afterward—in fact, until some time during the period of the Five Dynasties (907–960 A.D.) which preceded the Sung dynasty—it seems to have been the custom to furnish tombs of distinguished persons with a selection of ornaments, including models of their wives and concubines and personal possessions, such as saddle horses and oxcarts, as well as a variety of other articles for the use and comfort of the departed soul on its journey to the next world. Some of these things were of gold, silver, or bronze, but the majority were made of pottery of one sort or another (plates 13, 16, 18, and 19). For the greater part the pottery figures were of unglazed earthenware, usually undecorated but occasionally with colored decoration on a coating of white slip. However, in addition to the unglazed earthenware ornaments which were produced throughout the Han, North Wei, and Six Dynasties periods, a large quantity of rather crude pottery tomb-wares covered with a low-fired green glaze has been recovered from tombs of the Han dynasty (plates 11 and 12). They comprise figures of men and women, domestic animals of almost every kind, ornaments in the form of buildings, including watch towers and sheds for farm animals, candlesticks and other paraphernalia, and jars, dishes, and other utensils. In many cases the appearance of the excavated Han glazed wares is much enhanced by a silvery iridescence on the surface resulting from decomposition of the green glaze by the chemical action of the earth during the centuries of burial.

The T'ang dynasty witnessed a great increase in the national power of China, accompanied by an expansion of territory and a remarkable advance in learning and the arts. In particular, the manufacture of pottery surged forward, and a large number of kilns making a wide variety of different kinds of wares came into being. Of all the ceramics produced in the T'ang dynasty, best known are, no doubt, the three-color glazed tomb wares which will be considered later; but, technically speaking, the most advanced were the celadon wares of the Yüeh Chou kilns, which had been in operation at least since Six Dynasties times, and the white wares of Hsing Chou in the north of China. While Yüeh celadon of the T'ang period is by no means as plentiful as the well-known products of the Six Dynasties Chiu-yen kiln mentioned above, there is a fair number of pieces which clearly can be classed as Yüeh type and which stylistically belong to the T'ang period. A celadon jar bearing the date of the third year of Ch'ang Ching (corresponding to 823 A.D.), which was excavated some years ago from a site in Chekiang, has been of significant assistance in the identification of T'ang Yüeh ware.

[11]

Hsing Chou yao

According to Chinese tradition, the Hsing Chou kiln, whose products, in the words of an ancient Chinese record, were "white and soft as snow," was situated at Hsing tai near Nei ch'iu in Hopei province during the T'ang dynasty. Unfortunately, the kiln site remains undiscovered, so the identification of these famous wares is still in the realm of conjecture. However, it has become the fashion among connoisseurs of ceramics all over the world to give to white glazed wares with obvious T'ang characteristics the label "Hsing Chou type," and an example of one such attribution is a well-known ewer with phoenix head in the Tokyo National Museum. A fairly large number of white wares of a similar kind, comprising jars, vases, plates, ewers, and covered boxes, is known to exist (plates 22 and 23). They are characterized by a soft white pottery body covered with a white or creamy transparent glaze, and the bottom is usually flat.

Chi Chou yao

One of the most important of the T'ang period kilns was the Chi Chou yao, situated at Yung-ho, a village in the district of that name in the prefecture of Chi-an in Kiangsi province. During T'ang times the kiln is believed to have produced mainly white porcelaneous ware of fine quality, but unfortunately only very few pieces seem to have survived. The English scholar Brankston, who visited the site in 1938, discovered there a number of bluish-white fragments of a porcelaneous ware very similar in technique and appearance to the famous phoenix-headed ewer in the British Museum, which was thus identified as Chi Chou ware of the late T'ang or perhaps the Five Dynasties period. During Sung times the range of products of Chi Chou was apparently widened to include a number of different types of *temmoku* bowls as well as white glazed wares with incised decoration in the manner of Ting yao.

Kuang Chou yao

According to a Chinese literary reference of the T'ang period, white pottery wares made in Kwangtung were presented to the Court, and in a record of the T'ang dynasty preserved at the Ninwa temple in Kyoto there is also a mention of these Kwangtung wares in a somewhat unusual context. According to this reference, "when pottery wares are ground into powder for medicinal use, the most efficacious are the white wares of Kwangtung"—which seems to establish beyond reasonable doubt that white pottery was made there during the T'ang period, although up to the present there is no known means of identifying such ware. However, Professor Zao Sung-i of Hong Kong University, who carried out an investigation of ancient sites of pottery production in Kwangtung province some years ago, has recently reported that he discovered a large number of old kiln sites, probably datable to the T'ang dynasty, near the village of Pai yao at Chao Chou in Kwangtung province, and he concludes that this district was a large pottery-manufacturing center in T'ang times.

T'ang three-color glazed wares

The best-known of all T'ang pottery products are the famous three-color glazed wares which were manufactured for the ornamentation of tombs and which have consequently survived in relatively large numbers (plates 3, 4, 5 and 20). They are low-fired wares with glazes of straw color, amber, green, and blue, which are derivatives of the famous Han green lead glaze. The body is usually of pinkish, whitish, or light-buff earthenware, but occasionally one comes across three-color glazed ware with a harder red pottery body, and in this case the glazed decoration is applied on a coating of white slip. A theory has been advanced that the more common white-bodied wares were made in the vicinity of Lo-yang in Honan province and the superior quality articles with a hard red body at Chang-an in Shansi, but it seems more likely that these three-color wares were turned out in a number of other localities as well.

The form and decoration of many of the ceramic products of the T'ang period, and in particular the three-color glazed tomb pottery, were evidently much influenced by metal wares imported from the countries of the Near East. In particular, Persian and Sassanian influence appears to have been strong.

1. YÜEH-WARE CELADON JAR IN THE FORM OF A TOWER
EMBELLISHED WITH SCULPTURED FIGURES

Height, 13 3/8 in. Private Collection

Yüeh celadon ware, which first made its appearance toward the end of the Han period, was evidently turned out in large quantities and in a wide variety of shapes throughout the period of the Six Dynasties and in T'ang times at a number of places in the two provinces of Chekiang and Fukien. The ware is characterized by a brownish-green or grayish-green feldspathic glaze and is generally esteemed by connoisseurs as the precursor of all high-fired glazed pottery. The jar illustrated is considered to be an example of Yüeh ware of the Six Dynasties period from the "Nine Rocks" kiln, which was situated at Chiu-yen near Shaohsing in Chekiang. It is the best of its type in Japanese collections and is perhaps one of the finest in existence. The body is of gray semiporcelaneous stoneware covered with a dull brownish-green glaze with a fine crackle. The jar is roughly barrel-shaped and is surmounted by a tower with diminutive human figures around it and with a cover in the form of a roofed turret. Jars of this type have been excavated from a group of ancient tombs, including one reliably dated 282 A. D., in the neighborhood of Shao-hsing. It is thought that they were made to be buried with the dead as a refuge for the soul of the departed.

[14]

2. T'ANG GLAZED GLOBULAR JAR WITH DESIGN OF

GREEN AND WHITE MEDALLIONS

Height, 8 13/16 in. Diameter, 10 3/8 in. National Museum, Tokyo

One of the results of the great creative outburst which accompanied the T'ang cultural revival was the sudden appearance of a distinct type of pottery with a wide range of colored glazes previously unused. All these wares were made as tomb furniture, and consequently a very large number of pieces have survived in pristine condition. The body is almost always white or light buff in color, but occasionally examples may be seen where the clay is brownish or reddish. The jar illustrated belongs to the latter category, as it has a rare dark-red body. It is thought to be one of the earliest types of three-color glazed pottery. The form is very fine and the richly glazed abstract design is boldly applied in a manner typical of T'ang decorative art.

[16]

3. T'ANG THREE-COLOR GLAZED DEMON

Height, 42 in. Private Collection

The most eye-catching of all the objects in the enormous range of T'ang three-color glazed wares, which includes not only jars and other utensils but also a great variety of human and animal figures, are the grotesque demoniacal images, of which the example shown here is perhaps one of the finest in existence. These demons vary in size, but usually they are equipped with a lionlike head surmounted by a pair of horns, wings on the shoulders like Pegasus, and feet in the form of horses' hoofs. According to a surviving record of Han period customs, such strange, fabulous beasts represent a legendary guardian which the ancient Chinese believed would fly around the inside of a tomb with the object of deterring any inimical spirit which might arise from the dead. These pottery figures were placed on the coffin, therefore, to restrain the spirit of the dead from emerging to do harm to the living.

The opinion has been expressed that similar figures of demons were made as early as the Shang-Yin (1766–1122 B.C.) or Chou (1122–255 B.C.) periods. However, the known examples are mainly of the T'ang period, and the majority of these are of three-color glazed pottery.

[18]

4. T'ANG GLAZED GLOBULAR JAR WITH DAPPLED DECORATION

Height, 6 11/16 in. Diameter, 8 13/16 in. Private Collection

The beautiful jar illustrated here is believed to have been excavated near Lo-yang in Honan province, where there are innumerable remains of ancient tombs thought by some people to be those of the T'ang court and nobility. There are slight grounds for believing also that kilns which produced some of the T'ang glazed wares may actually have been situated in the vicinity of Mount Pei Nang Shan, some twenty miles to the northeast of Lo-yang, but the evidence is far from conclusive and no kiln site which can reliably be dated to the T'ang period has yet been discovered in the area.

The streaked and dappled effect, which is achieved by the application of the rich leaf-green and full amber yellow colors on the colorless wash glaze which covers this jar, achieves a delightful harmony rarely seen in such perfection even on other fine T'ang glazed wares.

7. T'ANG THREE-COLOR GLAZED LION

Height, 11 5/16 in. Hosokawa Collection, Tokyo

The extensive range of T'ang glazed animal figures already mentioned includes models of a legendary or fabulous lion of the type shown here, though compared with the numerous horses and camels they are relatively rare. This particular example is remarkable for the vigor of its execution and the expression of savage ferocity conveyed by the snarling mouth. The body is of whitish clay and the glaze is unusually thick and even.

There are in Japan about four or five other known examples of similar lions, including a well-known pair in the Seikado Foundation and one in the National Museum. Judging from the paucity of published examples, this type of glazed figure is rare also in European and American collections, although there was one formerly in the Oppenheim collection.

8. T'ANG WHITE GLOBULAR JAR

STREAKED WITH GREEN AND BLUE GLAZE

Height, 9 5/16 in. Diameter, 8 13/16 in. Private Collection

This is a remarkably beautiful example of a T'ang jar decorated with blue and green glaze. The loveliness of the gently swelling form is enhanced by the unrestrained flow of the glaze over the white undersurface.

As the body, quality of glaze, and potting show no significant departure from other T'ang glazed wares, it is inferred that this piece also comes from Lo-yang in Honan. While jars of this form with blue decoration on a white ground are not very unusual, those with mixed green and blue glaze are extremely rare, and, in fact, the only other example which comes to mind is a jar with cover from the St. Louis City Art Museum which was shown at the exhibition of antique Chinese pottery and porcelain at Los Angeles in 1952.

9. BLACK POTTERY MINIATURE FIGURES

Height, 2 3/8 in. to 3 3/8 in. Private Collection

These black pottery figures are said to be from a group of such objects which were excavated near Hui hsien in Honan in 1942 from a tomb site of the Warring States period. The whole of the black surface is smooth and shiny and gives the impression of having been polished. They are quite unlike any other early figures hitherto discovered, and if they are genuine (their authenticity is still in doubt) they represent the oldest known type of dancing figures. The rhythmical forms and great economy of line are extremely appealing, and in recent years they have come to be very much appreciated by lovers of modern art.

10. HAN POTTERY ACROBATS

Height, 2 1/2 in. to 3 1/4 in. Private Collection

The many charming varieties of Han pottery figures include models of scholars, musicians, dancers, and priests as well as of ordinary men and women. But these acrobats are unusually charming and full of humor. The body is a kind of dark-gray earthenware which was originally painted with white pigment, of which only the merest trace now remains.

11. HAN GREEN-GLAZED CANDLESTICK

Height, 20 ⁵/₈ in. Museum of the University of Tenri (Nara Prefecture)

For some years it was believed that the Han green-glazed wares represented the most ancient of Chinese glazed pottery, and indeed Professor Laufer went so far as to assert that a reference in Chinese records to the importation from the West of a kind of glasslike substance implied that ingredients for the glaze were imported from the West through Central Asia. Recently, however, glazed pots in a style unmistakably attributable to the Warring States period have been excavated at Lo-yang, and it is reported that the famous An-yang sites of the Shang-yin period have yielded pottery fragments with traces of glaze, so that it is evident that the Chinese made glazed pottery long before Han times.

Among the Han green-glazed wares which were all made as tomb furnishings, the most usual types besides jars, bowls, and other utensils are models of houses, farm buildings of various kinds, all sorts of farm animals, including pigs in pigsties, dogs, oxcarts, watch towers, and a host of other things. However, the candlestick illustrated here, which shows remarkable technical development, is possibly unique among Han green-glazed models. The body is reddish-brown earthenware covered with a low-fired green glaze which through decomposition has acquired an overall silver iridescence.

12. HAN GREEN-GLAZED "HILL JAR" INCENSE BURNER

Height, 8 13/16 in. Private Collection

The so-called hill jar type of incense burners was first produced during the Han dynasty, but evidently they were also made in large numbers throughout the Six Dynasties and T'ang periods. Their manufacture is related to the trade with the West and the South Seas which opened up during Han times and led to the import, among other things, of exotic kinds of incense, which in turn inspired potters to produce new types of incense burners. The "hill jars," which are described in detail in ancient Chinese records, seem to have been particularly popular, and it appears that the same form was reproduced in iron, bronze, stone, lacquer, and unglazed earthenware, but examples in green-glazed pottery are particularly numerous. The jars vary somewhat in form but basically have a dish-shaped base, a bowl on a high foot, and a pierced cover in the form of a hillock. The one illustrated here is somewhat unusual, as the cover is quite elaborately carved in relief. The body of this piece is of reddish earthenware, and it is covered with a low-fired green glaze which, as a result of decay during centuries of burial in the earth, has taken on a silvery iridescence. It is thought to have been excavated at Chang-an in Shansi.

13. SIX DYNASTIES FIGURE OF AN OFFICIAL

Height, 22 15/16 in. Private Collection

Although at first glance this pottery figure looks like a woman dressed in a long robe, it can be deduced that it is in fact intended to represent a court official. Dr. T. Kobayashi, in his book on Han and T'ang customs and tomb furnishings, tells us that men of a certain position customarily wore a high-crowned headdress and robes of the type shown in the illustration. Women usually had their hair extravagantly arranged and piled up high with a number of ornamental hairpins. Thus all the pottery models of human figures of the Han, Wei, and Six Dynasties periods with such tall hats may be taken to be male figures. People of those times, it seems, dressed with care and great elegance, and the elaborateness of the hair style and headdress increased in proportion to their social importance.

The long robe worn by the figure shown here is thought to be representative of the type of garment worn by both men and women during the period from Han times to the Six Dynasties. Judging from the general form, however, and in particular from the line of the body, which follows a convex curve from shoulder to foot, this figure is considered to date from about the end of the Six Dynasties period. The body is of dark-gray earthenware which was originally coated with a thin layer of white pigment and presumably decorated in color; but only traces of this pigment now remain.

14. SIX DYNASTIES POTTERY GUARDIAN

Height, 16 5/16 in. Private Collection

The helmeted and armored pottery figure shown here in the "ready" position as though to say, "Halt! Who goes there?" is of a type which was frequently placed in the four corners of tombs of the Six Dynasties period for the purpose of driving away evil spirits or malign influences. The head is disproportionately large, and the face is covered by a mask with gilded eyeballs. The arms evidently once held a halberd or a pike, and the whole body is covered by an extraordinary suit of heavy leather armor reinforced by another protective garment which appears to be made of some kind of metal. The material is the usual dark-gray, hard earthenware, and it may fairly be described as a remarkably fine example of a Six Dynasties period figure.

15. SIX DYNASTIES POTTERY FIGURE OF A PALACE GUARDIAN

Height, 16 1/4 in. Private Collection

Among Han and Six Dynasties pottery figures one occasionally sees fearsome-looking warriors with the left hand in the attitude of holding a shield and the right arm raised as though to throw a spear. The late Professor Laufer identified these as the "palace guardians" of the old Chinese legends. These beings were said to have worn headgear made of bearskin, gilded masks with four eyes, and black-and-red cloaks and to have carried spears and shields. With a hundred men under their command they were supposed to patrol the palace precincts three times a day at the hours when the evil spirits were deemed to be at their most powerful, and to drive away the malign influences. At burial ceremonies they were employed as escorts for the funeral cortège, and on arrival at the tomb it was their duty to enter and with their spears attack the four corners to destroy any evil spirits which might be lurking there. The figure illustrated with left arm crooked and right hand raised is no doubt intended to represent such a guardian. The spear and shield, being made of wood, have presumably rotted and disappeared. The body is the usual dark-gray earthenware common to figures of both the Han and Six Dynasties periods, but on general stylistic grounds this figure is considered to belong to the Six Dynasties period.

16. SIX DYNASTIES POTTERY HORSE

Height, 15 1/2 in. Hosokawa Collection, Tokyo

Early Chinese records indicate that fine horses were imported from the West in large numbers at least from early Han times. One such reference, dated 101 B.C., speaks of a certain Chinese traveler who returned from a visit to the lands of the Western barbarians with more than three thousand fleet steeds, and it can be taken that horses obtained with so much trouble and at such great expense must have been highly prized.

The horse illustrated here is perhaps the finest of the numerous surviving examples of pottery horses of the Han and Six Dynasties periods, and judging from the sturdy build, slender legs, and intrepid expression, the model for it must have been one of the fine imported thoroughbreds of which the old records speak. The clay has been sensitively handled and the final result is an object lesson in the possibilities of naturalistic modeling.

17. YÜEH YAO BLACK-GLAZED EWER

WITH CHICKEN-HEAD SPOUT

Height, 9 7/16 in. Diameter, 7 in. National Museum, Tokyo

This ewer is prized as a rare example of the earliest type of Oriental pottery with a high-fired black glaze. It was no doubt intended as a wine pourer, and the unusual shape is perhaps of ritualistic significance.

The body is of a hard, gray, ferruginous stoneware which has been thickly glazed with a brownish-black opaque glaze of feldspathic type, giving a mat surface. As may be seen from the illustration, the glaze is flaking off at several places, presumably because it was applied before the clay had fully dried out so that the fusion of body clay and glaze was incomplete.

In 1932 Mr. Yanaiyama, then the Japanese Consul at Hangchow, discovered a Six Dynasties kiln site near Tê-ch'ing in Chekiang province, and among the pottery shards which he collected there was one fragment of a black-glazed ewer with a chicken head, and sharp square loops on the shoulder almost exactly similar to the one illustrated. In 1955 Chinese Government archaeologists excavating tomb sites of the Six Dynasties period in the vicinity of Nanking unearthed a number of Yüeh-ware ewers with chicken-head spouts, among them at least two with black glaze of the type described above, one of which came from a tomb which according to their report can be reliably dated to the fifth century A.D. There are also two or three similar examples in collections in Japan and a few in European and American collections.

18.   T'ANG FIGURE OF A LADY

Height, 18 1/8 in.   Private Collection

The charming figure shown is of a delightfully buxom T'ang beauty wearing a loosely fitting robe and fondling a lap dog. In contrast to figures of the Six Dynasties period, which are, generally speaking, notably tall and spare of flesh, the T'ang figures tend to be well covered and of ample proportions, but the lady illustrated here is plump even by T'ang standards. It is related that a famous T'ang beauty named Yang Kuei Fei, who was afflicted with obesity, used to wear a special kind of wig or headdress in order to emphasize her pretty face, and it may be that the lady of our illustration is resorting to a similar artifice. According to ancient Chinese records, elaborate headdresses of this sort were much favored in T'ang China and in extreme cases were known to reach a height of nearly fourteen inches. This figure is of reddish-brown earthenware which was originally covered with a thin coating of white pigment, much of which, however, has peeled off over the centuries. Stout male figures made in a similar manner are not unknown but are very rare.

19. T'ANG UNGLAZED CAMEL WITH FOREIGN ATTENDANT

Height, 29 1/8 in. Length, 21 7/8 in. Private Collection

Although horses are the best known of T'ang pottery figures, the camels which are found in many different styles and sizes are also highly regarded, and surviving examples are almost equally numerous. In the example illustrated, which is of soft whitish clay modeled in a powerful manner showing great fire and spirit, there is an attendant mounted on the camel's back. Judging from his deep-set eyes and high-bridged nose, he is clearly intended to be a foreigner. It is noteworthy as an indication of the unrestricted foreign contacts made by China under the T'ang dynasty that many of the clay images of human figures depict foreign types; this camel attendant, modeled in an extraordinarily lifelike manner, is one of the finest of them all.

In T'ang China, foreigners from the West, among them Armenians, Greeks, Persians, and Hindus, were appointed to a number of official positions, including even the Imperial guards. This followed the submission of the Western barbarians to the Imperial power, a subject frequently depicted in T'ang paintings and scrolls, which led ultimately to a great enthusiasm for foreign importations of all sorts beginning in Chang-an and Lo-yang and extending throughout the length and breadth of the land. Not only did foreigners enter China in large numbers at this time but foreign manners and customs became very popular, and imported music, dancing, clothing, wine, and food enriched the daily life of the people.

20. T'ANG THREE-COLOR GLAZED LARGE DISH

WITH FLORAL DESIGN

Height, 4 5/8 in.   Diameter, 15 1/2 in.   Private Collection

This fine footed dish with boldly executed decoration conveys in a splendid manner the rich quality of T'ang art.

The body is pale buff in color, and the whole of the inside surface is covered with a bold floral motif in green, white, and amber glaze. The outside of the dish is amber-colored glaze flecked with white. The whole is mounted on a sturdy unglazed base.

A dish similar to this one was illustrated in the catalogue of the Eumorfopoulos collection and is now presumably housed in the British Museum, but no other example of a T'ang glazed dish is known to equal the piece shown here, which may be classed among the finest of T'ang glazed pottery. It was perhaps made at Lo-yang when the T'ang civilization was in full bloom, and like all other such T'ang pottery it was not intended for ordinary use but for the furnishing of a tomb.

21. T'ANG THREE-COLOR GLAZED DISH

WITH CONVENTIONALIZED FLOWER DESIGN

Height, 3 1/4 in. Diameter, 14 3/4 in. Private Collection

As an example of the finest quality of T'ang three-color glazed wares this large dish is in no way inferior to the piece illustrated in plate 20. The body is of the same soft, pale-buff clay and is decorated with a conventionalized flower design in white, green, and amber-colored glaze. The center pattern is incised under the glaze, as are the pleasing cloud motifs which surround it. This dish was exhibited together with a dish of very similar type from the Alfred Clark collection in the great exhibition of Chinese art held in London in 1935, but judging from the illustration of the latter in the catalogue of the exhibition the decoration does not quite come up to this one.

22. HSING CHOU WHITE POTTERY INKSTONE

Height, 2 5/8 in. Diameter, 7 3/4 in. Private Collection

The white wares of Hsing Chou, which were regarded in T'ang times as being of equal merit with the Yüeh celadons, are thought to have been made in the neighborhood of Hsing tai in Hopei province. An old kiln site was discovered in the area in 1941, but subsequent investigations have shown that it dates only from Ming times, and the precise location of the T'ang period kilns which produced this white-bodied ware still remains unknown. It is therefore not possible to say for sure whether the type of ware which we call Hsing Chou yao does in fact correspond to the famous T'ang white ware described in the old records. However, from the fact that pottery of this type, demonstrating unmistakable T'ang features, has been excavated in quantities at various places in Hopei and Honan provinces, there are reasonable grounds for assuming that it does. A number of American and European scholars, among them the Swedish Dr. Lindberg, are believed to share this opinion.

The inkstone illustrated, which is considered to be Hsing Chou ware, is somewhat unusual, although there is a piece of much the same shape preserved in the Domeiji temple in Osaka which was probably taken to Japan several centuries ago.

Occasionally T'ang three-color glazed inkstones of similar shape may be seen, and in Japan the same form occurs in inkstones of Sueki wares of the Nara period (eighth century A.D.). This one is expertly potted and altogether of great technical excellence, as befits a fine piece of T'ang Hsing Chou ware.

23. T'ANG WHITE EWER OF GLOBULAR FORM

Height, 8 13/16 in.   Diameter, 6 13/16 in.   Private Collection

While this ewer cannot be positively identified as Hsing Chou yao, in quality of body, texture and color of glaze, and technique of potting, it exhibits many of the same features as may be seen in the inkstone shown in plate 22. The porcelaneous body is almost pure white and is covered to within 1 3/16 inches of the foot with a translucent semi-mat white glaze which is very finely crazed. The lower part of the globe of the ewer is unglazed. The handle, short spout, and swelling globular form are all characteristically T'ang in execution, and it may perhaps be described as a typical T'ang ewer although the form exhibits strong Western influence. It may have been intended as a container for "foreign wine." Similar pieces are not unknown, but the balanced shape and restrained beauty of this piece give it special distinction.

24. WHITE POTTERY COVERED BOX

WITH MOTH DECORATION

Height, 1 7/16 in. Diameter, 1 3/4 in. Hakone Art Museum

This covered box of typical T'ang form has a decorative lid with a moth (or perhaps a butterfly) molded under the glaze. The ware is possibly Hsing Chou yao, but in comparison with the white inkstone and the ewer shown in plates 22 and 23 the color and texture of the glaze seem different. An interesting feature of this little box is the use of "iron" spots for decorative effect. Although the object is probably of T'ang date, it could conceivably be somewhat later—perhaps Five Dynasties. One or two similar examples are known to exist, but this one is particularly pleasing.

25. YÜEH CELADON COVERED BOX

Height, 2 5/16 in. Diameter, 4 3/4 in. Hakone Art Museum

The covered box illustrated here is a charming example of the famous T'ang Yüeh ware. The Yüeh kiln site was first discovered in 1930 on the edge of Shang Lin Lake near Yü yao in Chekiang, and a great many pottery shards which were picked up on the site were taken to Japan. Interestingly, several hundreds of shards of exactly similar type have recently been excavated from ancient burial sites in Japan (mainly at Heiwa Dai near Fukuoka in Kyushu), though in this case perfect pieces were few in number.

Although examples of Yüeh ware of the T'ang period are fairly numerous, artistically carved pieces of the type here illustrated are extremely rare, in fact, there are no more than two or three known in Japanese collections. The body is of dark-gray ferruginous clay covered all over with a dark-olive transparent glaze under which can be seen the carved decoration associated with Yüeh. The shape is distinctive, and the beautifully made high foot is characteristically T'ang in style.

26. T'ANG DARK-BROWN GLAZED JAR

Height, 11 7/16 in. Diameter 11 in. Hakone Art Museum

This is a truly great pot, and it is evident that much care was lavished in the making of it. The four pairs of ears on the shoulder are an unusual feature, and the great swelling body decorated with bold lotus petals carved in relief is a highly original form. Compared with the relatively numerous celadon and white wares, dark-brown glazed T'ang pottery of this sort is rare. Judging from the way the foot is made and from the general style, there is little doubt that this piece dates from the T'ang period, although it cannot yet be positively identified with any particular kiln.

Jars of similar form with ears grouped in four pairs have been excavated from Shang-Yin sites at An-yang, so it may be inferred that the form goes back at least to the tenth century B. C.

SUNG POTTERY AND PORCELAIN

GENERAL

DURING the Sung dynasty the art of the Chinese potter, which had its beginnings in Han and Six Dynasties times and flowered vigorously during the T'ang period, reached its zenith. The succeeding Yüan period marked a decline in the technique of pottery manufacture and, although there was a splendid renaissance in the Ming period and subsequently for a short time in the eighteenth century, the product never again reached the technical and artistic level achieved by the Sung potters, especially those of the "Golden Age" at the end of the Northern Sung period (960–1126 A.D.).

The Sung period was one of grand and singular achievement in philosophy and the arts, and the cultured Chinese of the day had a great taste for antiquarian and literary pursuits, which led to a demand for porcelain wares imitating the highly prized jade and in the style and form of the classic bronzes of antiquity. This demand spurred the production of stone-wares and porcelaneous wares, which were now made to an extent which as far as our present knowledge goes had never before been attempted. The feldspathic glazes used had been developed by a slow process of trial and error into dense, hard, vitreous coverings of a kind previously unknown in ceramic art. Among kilns which produced these superb wares in great quantities in both North and South China in Sung times some of the most famous are those of Ting, Ju, Tung, Chün, Tz'ŭ Chou, Lung-ch'üan, Chien, and Ching-tê-chên, and a surprisingly large number of the masterpieces which they turned out have come down to us through the centuries. In general these Sung wares are characterized by an elegant simplicity and great vigor. They are notable for their refinement of form and for a fine quality of compactness and restraint in the decoration, where it occurs. A large proportion, however, are undecorated and rely for effect solely on the noble shapes and the smooth jewel-like surface of the colored glazes.

HISTORICAL BACKGROUND OF POTTERY PRODUCTION IN SUNG TIMES

The first Sung emperor, on ascending the throne, enthusiastically set about encouraging education as part of a national policy which had as its object the ending of the domination of affairs by the warrior class, for centuries a deep-rooted evil in Chinese society. This policy was continued by succeeding Sung rulers, who held steadfastly to the political ideal of efficient and honest civil administration throughout the three hundred years of Sung rule. A remarkable advance in learning and ultimately in the cultural level of the people as a whole resulted. Arts and literature made rapid progress, owing in part to a development in the art of printing, which allowed a wider public access to books, and the way was opened for the ordinary people to enter government service. At the same time there was a widespread increase in commerce, which was accompanied by a considerable rise in the living standards of the common people. The main philosophical trend of the time was based on Confucianism, and many great Confucian scholars were invited to the Court to take part in government and to guide public morals, with the result that the Confucian philosophy gradually came to color every aspect of the life of the people. Buddhism, which had degenerated in China by Sung times, was no longer popular, but the profound philosophy of the Zen sect appealed strongly to the intellectuals. The reflection of both these philosophies may be seen in the Sung pottery wares, which in general display elegance, compactness, sincerity, and purity.

THE DEVELOPMENT OF COMMERCE AND INDUSTRY

From earliest times in China there was a discernible tendency to despise commerce and make light of merchants; for example, before the Sung dynasty very little provision seems to have been made in town planning for the accommodation of merchants. But with the Sung reforms large trading concerns came into being, a new standard currency was brought into circulation throughout the country, and a system of negotiable money-orders was introduced; in fact, the entire economic system underwent a complete change, with the result that commerce increased astonishingly, and a marked rise in the social status of the merchant class followed. Existing restrictions on traffic between the various sections of the towns were lifted; music halls, theaters, brothels, and other places of public entertainment sprang up one after another, and shops were drastically modernized. At Kaifeng, the capital, the business sections of the city are said to have expanded beyond the outer walls, and numbers of shops, restaurants, teahouses, and places of entertainment stood in rows before the main gates. This flourishing condition of commerce brought about a greatly increased demand for all sorts of handicrafts, including textiles, pottery, lacquer ware, paper, Chinese ink, and wax candles; and Marco Polo in his book of travels in Asia records the opinion that the technical level of handicrafts in Cathay was far higher than anything to be seen in major Italian towns and cities. During the second half of the Northern Sung period the output of pottery and stoneware must have been enormous, and the finer of the ceramic products were prized by people in all levels of society from the merchants to the nobility and the Emperor himself.

SUNG EXPORT WARES

The flourishing export trade which developed during Sung times also served to promote the production of pottery and porcelain. To supplement the ancient overland route, a large number of ports were opened for foreign vessels, which came from as far away as Arabia and Persia, bringing such desirable merchandise as pearls, ivory, rhinoceros horn, camphor, olibanum, agallochum, coral, emeralds, agate, and medicines of various sorts. In exchange, China exported silk, lacquer ware, and ceramics. The enormous quantity of Sung pottery articles and fragments which have been excavated in Indo-China, Thailand, Malaya, and the Philippines, as well as in Persia, Egypt, and elsewhere in the Middle East, testifies to the wide scale of the export trade in pottery at this time. There is abundant evidence that ceramic wares were brought into Japan in great quantities during Sung times. Among these, celadon wares and *ch'ing-pai* or *ying ch'ing* (shadow blue) wares were particularly numerous and quantities of the latter in the form of small pots and covered boxes, besides thousands of shards, have been found in Japanese tombs datable to the Fujiwara period (897–1185 A.D.).

SOME OBSERVATIONS ON SUNG KILNS

There are marked differences between the wares of North and South China, both in technique of manufacture and in form and decoration. In general, the Sung kilns of North China specialized in the production of stonewares, while those of South China produced vitreous pottery and true porcelain. In North China, where the kilns were built up on level ground, coal was burned as fuel and the pots were fired with an oxidizing flame. In South and Central China, however, where wood fuel was used, the system was to build kilns on the slope of a hill so as to ensure a forced draft and to fire the pots by a reduction process. In South China, moreover, the glaze was applied directly to the clay body and then fired, while in the North, with certain exceptions, the system was to apply a coat of white slip to the body and then glaze over it. With respect to form, as a broad generalization it may be said that while the wares of North China frequently show signs of strong Western—particularly Persian—influence, those of the South are peculiarly Chinese.

In addition to these regional variations, there is also a marked difference between the wares made during the Northern Sung (960–1126 A.D.) period and the later wares of the Southern

Sung (1127–1279) time, in that the former tend to be more powerful in form and more vigorous in decoration. However, the Southern Sung wares are by no means lacking in vigor; they are noted for their elegance, and the quality of the body and perfection of the glazes of ceramics of that period have never been surpassed.

In Japan it is usual to consider the masterpieces of the Northern Sung epoch (plates 28, 29, 30, 35, 36, 37, 38, 39, 40, 41, 42, 43, 44, 45, and 46) as reflecting the spirit of Confucianism; and those of the Southern Sung, which include a number of articles, such as incense burners, vases, and offertory bowls, clearly intended for use as Buddhist altar fittings (plates 32, 33, 48, and 49), as embodying the spirit of the Zen sect of Buddhism. The material differences between the wares of the two periods may easily be noted by comparing the Ting wares (plates 35 and 36) and the Northern celadons (plates 38 and 39)—representative products of the Northern Sung period—with such typically Southern Sung wares as Lung-ch'üan celadons (plate 49) and Southern Sung Kuan yao (plates 32 and 48).

The total number of kilns in operation during the Sung dynasty must have been vast indeed, but our knowledge of the subject is still only fragmentary, and so it is frequently impossible to identify the kiln which produced a specific piece of pottery, and even where Sung kiln sites have been discovered it by no means follows that they were the sole source of any one type of ware. In fact, judging from the evidence of Lung-ch'üan, where it is known that in Sung times great numbers—perhaps running into hundreds—of kilns were located, all producing much the same sort of celadon wares, it is likely that the several known types of Sung ceramics were turned out by many different kilns and perhaps even in widely separated localities.

Of the great number of Sung dynasty kilns mentioned in literary references the following, listed with their locations, are some of the more famous:

Ting	Hopei Province	(North China)
Tz'ū Chou	Hopei Province	(North China)
Northern Sung Kuan	Honan Province	(North China)
Tung	Honan Province	(North China)
Ju	Honan Province	(North China)
Chün	Honan Province	(North China)
Yüeh Chou	Chekiang Province	(Central China)
Lung-ch'üan	Chekiang Province	(Central China)
Hsiu-nei-ssu Kuan	Chekiang Province	(Central China)
Chiao t'an Kuan	Chekiang Province	(Central China)
Chi Chou	Kiangsi Province	(Central China)
Ching-tê-chên	Kiangsi Province	(South China)
Chien	Fukien Province	(South China)

The actual sites of many of these kilns remain unidentified, but the present Chinese Government is actively encouraging scientific excavation and since about 1952 Chinese scholars are reported to have discovered a large number of sites associated with the Sung period, so there is a good chance that our knowledge will be enlarged in the near future. Up to the present, however, few detailed reports on this subject have been published by the scholars concerned.

27. TING WHITE BOWL WITH GILDED DECORATION

OF FLYING CRANES AND CLOUDS

Diameter, 6 1/8 in. Private Collection

Ting ware is a product of one of the most famous of the kilns of the Northern Sung period (960–1126 A. D.). The kiln site was discovered near a village called Ch'ientzu at Shêngyang in Honan Province, and it is thought that the kiln may date from an earlier time—perhaps as early as T'ang. Certainly the Ting kilns were flourishing toward the end of the Northern Sung period, when they were turning out white glazed wares of extraordinary beauty, some quite plain but a large proportion with decoration incised or molded under the glaze. The bowl illustrated here, however, is of a very rare type, as the decoration was applied over the glaze—in gilt. Only traces of the gilding now remain, but the imprint of the design is to be seen on the surface of the glaze. The shape of this bowl, which is said to have been excavated from a tomb in Korea during the twenties, is very elegant and the potting of the small foot particularly fine. The color is rather whiter than most Ting wares, which have a distinctive ivory tint, and the transparent glaze covers the lip. The lower part of the outside of the bowl and the foot are left unglazed.

28. CHÜN WARE DISH WITH PURPLE SPLASHES

Height, 1 3/16 in. Diameter, 7 1/16 in. Private Collection

The potteries of Chün Chou (the modern Jü Hsien) in Honan are believed to have been started early in the Sung dynasty and to have continued working well into the Ming period. However, from the fact that the surviving examples of Chün pottery display a great many variations of body and glaze it seems evident that the same type of ware was also made elsewhere in Honan and probably in other provinces of China as well.

The dish illustrated is usually considered one of the best examples of Chün ware in Japan. It has a soft, blue, semiopaque glaze with markings of a subdued reddish-purple color over a buff stoneware body left bare at the foot, where it is burned to a red-brown. The potting of this type of Chün ware has many features in common with the so-called Northern celadons (plates 12 and 13), and it is believed that Jü Hsien was the main production center for both groups.

29. GREEN-GLAZED TZ'Ū CHOU-TYPE VASE

WITH PEONY DESIGN IN BLACK

Height, 9 2/1 in. Private Collection

Tz'ū Chou-type vases of this typically Northern Sung shape with flower designs painted in black or brown on a white slip are well known, but those with a green-glazed body are much less common. This vase, which is considered to be one of the best examples in Japan, has a body of reddish-buff stoneware and a bold black design of a peony and foliage. To produce this effect the body was first covered with a white slip and the peony design applied in ferruginous enamel under a transparent glaze, after which it was fired in the ordinary way at about 1200–1300 degrees centigrade. Later the vase was covered all over with a "lower temperature" green glaze and refired at about 900 degrees. This accounts for the degraded state of the green glaze which, being fired at a lower temperature, has not fused with the body and has suffered considerable decomposition during the centuries of burial.

30.   TZ'Ū CHOU *MEI P'ING* VASE WITH DESIGN OF PEONIES

Height, 16 in. Hosokawa Collection, Tokyo

This *mei p'ing* vase is one of the more famous of Sung ceramics in Japan. The incised design of peony scrolls forming eight lozenges reserved in black on the milk-white background is particularly well balanced and graceful, and the elegant form is expressive of the great refinement of the Northern Sung age. It was perhaps made at Tang yang yū in Hsiu wu hsien, Honan Province, where, according to a report of Dr. Karlbeck, a large group of kilns was active in Northern Sung times turning out superior wares of the Tz'ū Chou type.

31. TZ'Ŭ CHOU-TYPE BOWL WITH FLORAL DECORATION IN COLORED ENAMELS

Height, 2 1/16 in.   Diameter, 5 7/8 in.   Private Collection

Overglaze decoration in colored enamels appears to have been devised for the first time toward the end of the Sung dynasty and evidently found immediate favor, judging from the numerous fragments which have been discovered on sites in North China and more particularly in Mongolia, considered to be of the Sung and Yüan periods. The bowl with peony design illustrated here gives a good idea of the color of this earliest enameled ware, which is highly regarded in Japan, where it is known as *"Sōakae"* (Sung red picture ware). It is a reddish or buff stoneware coated with a milk-white slip and covered with transparent glaze, after which it is fired. Subsequently the decoration is added over the glaze in red and green enamels, and finally the piece is refired, this time at a lower temperature.

In 1127 the Emperor Hui-tsung of the Sung dynasty was driven from his capital by the Chin (Nü-chên) Tartar invasion from the northwest. Thereafter all China north of the Yangtse River came under the domination of the Tartars, while the Sung court re-established itself in a new southern capital, first at Nanking and afterwards in the vicinity of the modern Hangchow.

Several examples of *Sōakae* bowls are known with dates of the Chin (Nü-chên) Tartar dynasty, inscribed in ink on the unglazed base. One of the inscriptions is of the first year of T'ai-ho (1201) and the other the seventh year of Chêng-tai (1250).

32. HSIU-NEI-SSŪ KUAN YAO CELADON

Height, 7 1/16 in. Nezu Art Gallery, Tokyo

This Southern Sung vase from the Nezu collection is famous in Japan for its flawless form and the serene bluish-green color of the celadon glaze. It appears to be of different technique from the Lung-ch'üan celadons, which are the type most numerous in Japan, and it is generally inferred from the potting of the base that it is a product of the Hsiu-nei-ssū yao, the Kuan (Imperial or official) ceramic factory of the Southern Sung court when the capital was established at Hangchow.

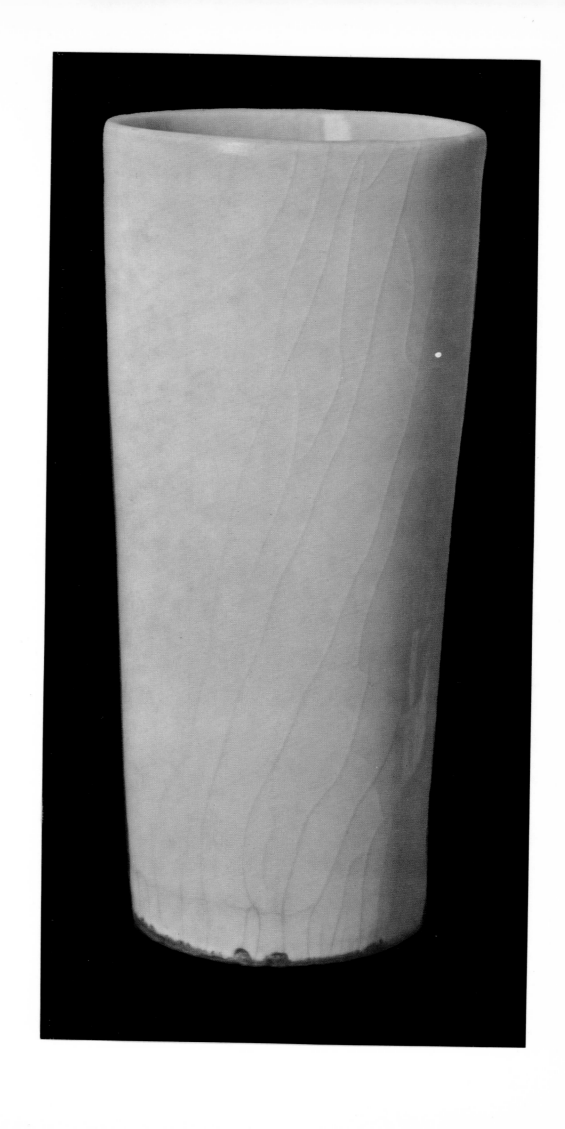

33. CHIEN-WARE "YAO PIEN" *TEMMOKU* TEA BOWL

KNOWN BY THE NAME "INABA"

Height, 2 8/5 in. Diameter, 4 3/4 in. Seikado Foundation, Tokyo

This is the most celebrated of three famous tea bowls of the type termed "yao pien" *temmoku,* which have been preserved in Japan by the tea masters as objects of great admiration, amounting almost to veneration, for centuries. It was sold at auction in 1917 for the fabulous sum of 168,000 yen, equivalent at that time to about $42,000, the highest price ever recorded in Japan for a piece of pottery. The interior of the bowl is thickly covered with an intense black *temmoku* glaze which is dotted over-all with rounded spots of various sizes gleaming with dark-blue, bluish-green, lapis lazuli, and silver iridescence. The exterior is also covered with a lustrous black glaze, but the foot is unglazed and reveals a dark-brown, highly ferruginous stoneware body characteristic of Chien wares. The term "yao pien" is thought to refer to the kiln transmutation, presumably quite fortuitous, which produced the exquisite iridescence in the glaze.

34. CHI CHOU *TEMMOKU* TEA BOWL WITH LEAF DESIGN

Height, 2 in. Diameter, 5 7/8 in. Private Collection

Introduced here is another type of *temmoku* tea bowl which is highly prized by Japanese devotees of the tea ceremony. It is considered to be a product of the Chi Chou kilns, which have a history going back to T'ang times, and was probably made during the Southern Sung period and taken to Japan shortly afterward. The potting is relatively thick and the form is characteristic of Chi Chou ware. The body is grayish-white, covered with a brownish-black mat glaze, and the leaf design appears to have been effected by firing the bowl with an actual leaf placed on the glaze surface. Such tea bowls as this are rarely met with outside Japan, where, however, there are a fair number—at least twenty or thirty good examples are known—which have been preserved for centuries for use in the tea ceremony.

35. TING YAO BLACK SHALLOW BOWL

WITH GILDED DECORATION OF FLOWERS

Height, 2 1/16 in. Diameter, 7 7/16 in. Hakone Art Museum

The name "Ting yao" is usually associated with the ivory-colored wares of that type which exist in great numbers, but the Ting kilns also produced a relatively small quantity of reddish-brown glazed wares (known in Japan as "persimmon *temmoku*") and perhaps an even smaller number of black-glazed pieces with a high gloss like black lacquer, which are known generally as "black Ting." The example illustrated is of this kind but shows traces of having been additionally decorated with a design of flowers applied in gold leaf to the inside glaze surface. It is said to have been excavated in Korea from a Koryō dynasty tomb, and the possibility exists, of course, that the gilding was done either in Korea or in China after the bowl left the Ting factory. This piece commands great admiration and has recently been designated an Important Cultural Property.

36. TING YAO LARGE BOWL WITH INCISED DESIGN OF LOTUSES

Height, 4 7/16 in. Diameter, 15 3/4 in. Hakone Art Museum

The large bowl illustrated here is a representative example of the best quality of Ting ware, which was produced in large quantities at Ting Chou in Chihli Province during the Northern Sung period. The ware evidently enjoyed a great contemporary vogue, and there are many favorable references to it in the old Chinese literary records. It has always been highly regarded in Japan, too, and a number of pieces are known which must have been introduced from China several hundred years ago and have been handed down through several generations of Japanese to the present day. Such pieces are known in Japan as *densei hin*.

This footed bowl has the usual Ting opaque white porcelain body covered with a transparent glaze with no trace of crackle. The inside surface is decorated with a conventionalized pattern of lotuses incised in the clay under the glaze in the free-flowing manner characteristic of Ting wares, and the outside is plain but with indentations which create a petal-like effect. In common with all other known Ting bowls of this type, the glaze stops just short of the rim, where the plain white body is exposed. This bowl is generally considered to be among the finest examples of Ting ware in Japan.

37. JU-WARE DISH

Height, 13/16 in. Diameter, 6 7/8 in. Private Collection

The famous twelfth-century Imperial ware made at Ju Chou (the modern Lin-ju Hsien) remained unidentified until recent years, but in 1936 the subject was exhaustively studied by Sir Percival David, and it is now generally agreed by scholars of Chinese ceramics that Ju ware may be identified with fair certainty as a sharply potted, yellowish-buff, porcelaneous stoneware with a smooth dense glaze, sometimes but not always crackled, of a light greenish-blue. The colors may vary considerably, some specimens being almost the "peacock-green" color of the finest Korean celadons and others approaching sky blue. The Imperial kiln at Ju Chou is thought to have been started in 1107 and must have closed down after the flight of the Sung court to the south in 1127, so that it had a relatively short life, which may account in part for the extreme rarity of Ju ware today. In Japan, at any rate, despite the great variety and large quantity of excellent Sung wares in private and public collections, it was not possible to point to an example of Ju ware until very recently, when the dish illustrated here was discovered. This piece has all the characteristics of Ju mentioned above, and the rounded potting of the foot is reminiscent of early Sung Yüeh ware, which is believed to have had certain features in common with Ju. The color is green with a hint of blue, and the glaze is covered with a fine crackle.

[88]

38. NORTHERN CELADON VASE WITH ENGRAVED DESIGN OF PEONIES AND ORNAMENTAL FOLIAGE

Height, 11 7/16 in. Hakone Art Museum

The vase illustrated here is a superb example of the so-called Northern celadon wares, which are thought to have been made at Ju Chou in Honan province during the Northern Sung dynasty. The body, which is of ferruginous buff stoneware burned brown where it is exposed at the foot, is covered with an olive-colored semitransparent glaze, and the elaborate design of peonies and ornamental foliage is skillfully carved in relief under the glaze.

While Northern celadon wares in the form of bowls and dishes are quite numerous, examples of vases are extremely rare—in fact, there are probably not more than half a dozen in the world—and this piece must be counted one of the best of them.

39. NORTHERN CELADON PILLOW

WITH ENGRAVED DESIGN OF PHOENIX AND PEONIES

Length, 9 1/4 in. Seikado Foundation (former Iwasaki Collection), Tokyo

It is apparent from the relatively large number of examples which have been excavated that the Chinese of Sung times had a predilection for pillows of pottery and porcelain. Pillows of white Tz'ū Chou ware with black painted decoration are especially numerous, but considerable numbers of Sung three-color glazed pottery pillows and, more rarely, Ting-type white-ware and Northern celadon ones are also to be seen.

The pillow illustrated here is not only one of the most beautiful of all but also perhaps the finest example of Northern celadon ware in existence. It is exquisitely carved all over in relief with a sophisticated design of a phoenix and conventionalized peonies, and covered with a semitransparent grayish-olive glaze. The base is flat and unglazed, exposing the buff-colored stoneware body.

40. CHING-TÊ-CHÊN "CH'ING-PAI" COVERED BOWL

AND SAUCER IN THE FORM OF A LOTUS

Diameter of saucer, 7 11/16 in. Seikado Foundation (former Iwasaki Collection), Tokyo

Porcelain ware of this type is commonly known as *ying ch'ing* (shadow blue). It is a thin translucent white porcelain burning to a faintly reddish color where the body is exposed to the fire, and it is frequently decorated with lightly incised engraving in relief and covered with a clear bluish or greenish glaze. This glaze color is naturally deepest in the grooves and incisions where the glaze has pooled, which gives rise to the name "shadow blue." Despite the fact that the ware has a rather fragile appearance, surprisingly large quantities of it have survived and are to be found in collections in Europe and America as well as in Japan, where many examples of a fairly coarse quality have been excavated from tombs of the Fujiwara period (897-1185 A.D.).

This rare covered bowl, which is of particularly fine quality as regards both potting and form, was perhaps intended as an offertory furnishing for a Buddhist altar. The saucer is in the shape of a fully opened lotus, and the bowl and cover represent a lotus bud about to burst into flower.

[95]

41. CHING-TÊ-CHÊN "CH'ING-PAI" EWER

Height, 7 1/4 in. Diameter, 6 7/16 in. Private Collection

The ewer illustrated is another example of the well-known *ying ch'ing* ware (see note on plate 40), of the Northern Sung dynasty. The potting is extremely thin and light, and the form and decoration demonstrate great technical skill in the handling of the fine porcelain clay. The spout and handle in particular are most delicately molded. The glaze, which is covered with a fine crackle, is almost color-less, so that in appearance the ewer is nearly pure white. The base is unglazed.

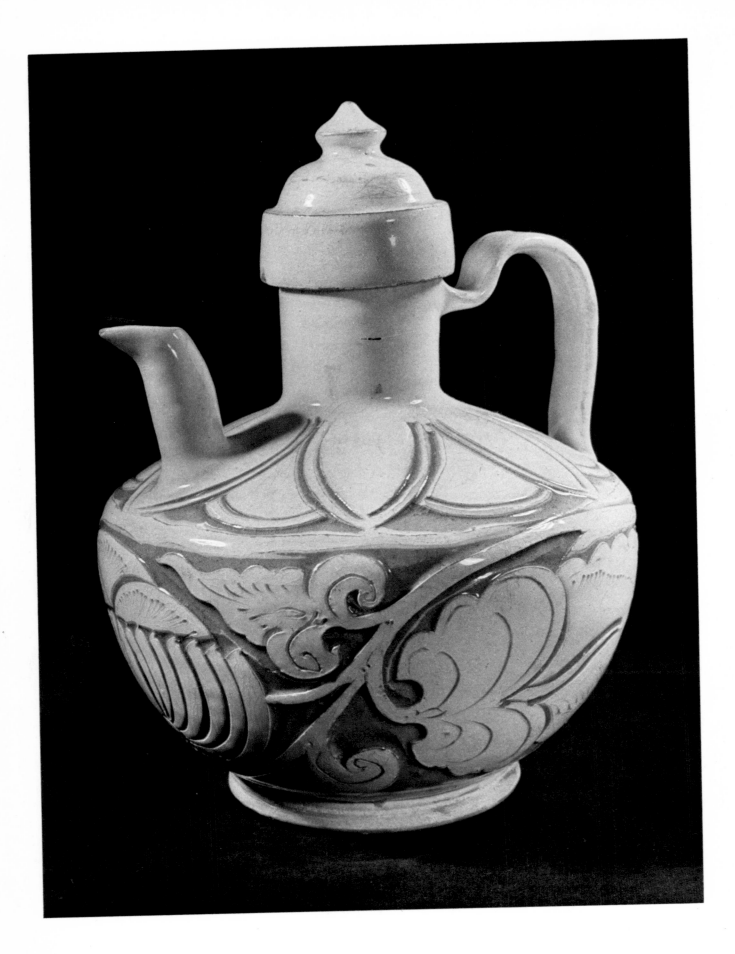

42. TZ'Ū CHOU-TYPE EWER WITH *SGRAFFITO* DECORATION

OF PEONY SCROLLS

Height, 8 1/16 in.   Diameter, 7 1/8 in.   National Museum, Tokyo

Shown here is one of the best pieces of Tz'ū Chou-type *sgraffito* ware existing in Japan. It is a hard, grayish-white, porcelaneous stoneware covered with a thick white slip, which has been scraped off to leave a design of peony scrolls carved in deep relief around the sides with a band of petals engraved around the neck. The surface is covered with a semitransparent, soft, white glaze which presents a high luster, and the areas where the white slip is retained under the glaze show a soft milk-white texture. This Tz'ū Chou ewer is famous all over the world among con- noisseurs of Chinese ceramics.

43. WHITE "MARBLED WARE" TEA BOWL

Height, 2 7/16 in. Diameter, 4 1/8 in. Hakone Art Museum

Among the ceramic wares roughly classified as Tz'ū Chou type may be included a class of "marbled ware" of the kind represented by the bowl illustrated here. This type of ware was produced in China at least as early as the T'ang dynasty, and there is a theory that it may have been inspired by a ceramic technique used in ancient Roman pottery. It is made by kneading together clays of different colors, rather in the manner of pastry-making, to create patterns resembling overlapping clouds, wood grain, or, as in the case of this little bowl, a basketwork effect. The mouth rim of this piece is painted with white slip, and a transparent white glaze is applied to the whole surface. The base is flat and there is no foot.

44. TZ'Ŭ CHOU *MEI P'ING* VASE WITH BLACK DRAGON DESIGN

Height, 16 in. Diameter, 8 3/8 in. Hakutsuru Museum, Kobe

Dragon designs in Chinese art are seen in their earliest form on archaic ritual bronzes of the Shang-Yin period, and thereafter the dragon motif occupies a significant position in Chinese art history; but few examples are so perfect in composition and in graphic representation as the design on this famous *mei p'ing* vase. It has the hard, grayish, porcelaneous body usually associated with Sung Tz'ū Chou wares of the best quality, covered all over with a creamy-white slip. The dragon decoration is applied on this surface with a solid coat of ferruginous black clay subsequently incised to reveal the creature's scaly body and other features, and the whole is covered with a transparent glaze showing traces of crackle from deterioration during the centuries of burial in the earth. From every aspect the design presents a flawless composition, and the vase as a whole proudly demonstrates the powerful quality of Northern Sung decorative art.

Another Tz'ū Chou vase with a dragon design even larger than this is in the Kansas City Museum.

45. TZ'Ū CHOU *MEI P'ING* VASE WITH DESIGN OF PEONIES

Height, 13 in. Private Collection

There is very little to be said about this magnificent *mei p'ing* vase, which speaks for itself. The sheer audacity and perfect balance of the bold peony design leave the beholder breathless. The body, glaze, and method of manufacture are the same as described in the notes to plates 42 and 44.

46. TZ'Ū CHOU LARGE BLACK-AND-WHITE JAR
WITH DESIGN OF FLOWERS AND BIRDS

Height, 9 7/16 in. Hosokawa Collection, Tokyo

This beautifully decorated black-and-white jar is of a form seldom seen among surviving examples of Tz'ū Chou ware. The body and the technique of decoration and glazing are the same as described in the notes to plates 42 and 44. The design on the reverse side is of a bird perched on the branch of a plum tree. The whole jar is in almost pristine condition, and it is hard to believe that it was buried in the ground for upwards of eight hundred years. It was formerly owned by Mr. Henri Rivière of Paris but was acquired by a Japanese buyer early in the thirties.

[107]

47. HONAN *TEMMOKU* BOTTLE VASE

Height, 8 1/4 in. Private Collection

Vases of this form with a small neck and mouth on wide shoulders with a truncated body are known in Japan as *toropin* and are greatly sought after. This one is a particularly fine example of the so-called Honan *temmoku* wares with glossy black glaze and a decoration of iron-brown splashes, which have been excavated in quantities from tomb sites of the Sung period at a number of widely distributed places in Honan Province and elsewhere in North China. Vases and bowls of this type have also been found in Korean tombs of the Koryō dynasty. The body is a hard, gray, porcelaneous ware covered with a highly lustrous black glaze which in turn is decorated with the typical reddish-brown iron splashes. Scholars of ceramics are not yet in complete agreement about the probable location of the kiln which produced wares of this type in Sung times, but, on the face of it, it seems likely that they were made at a number of different places in the general area of Honan Province.

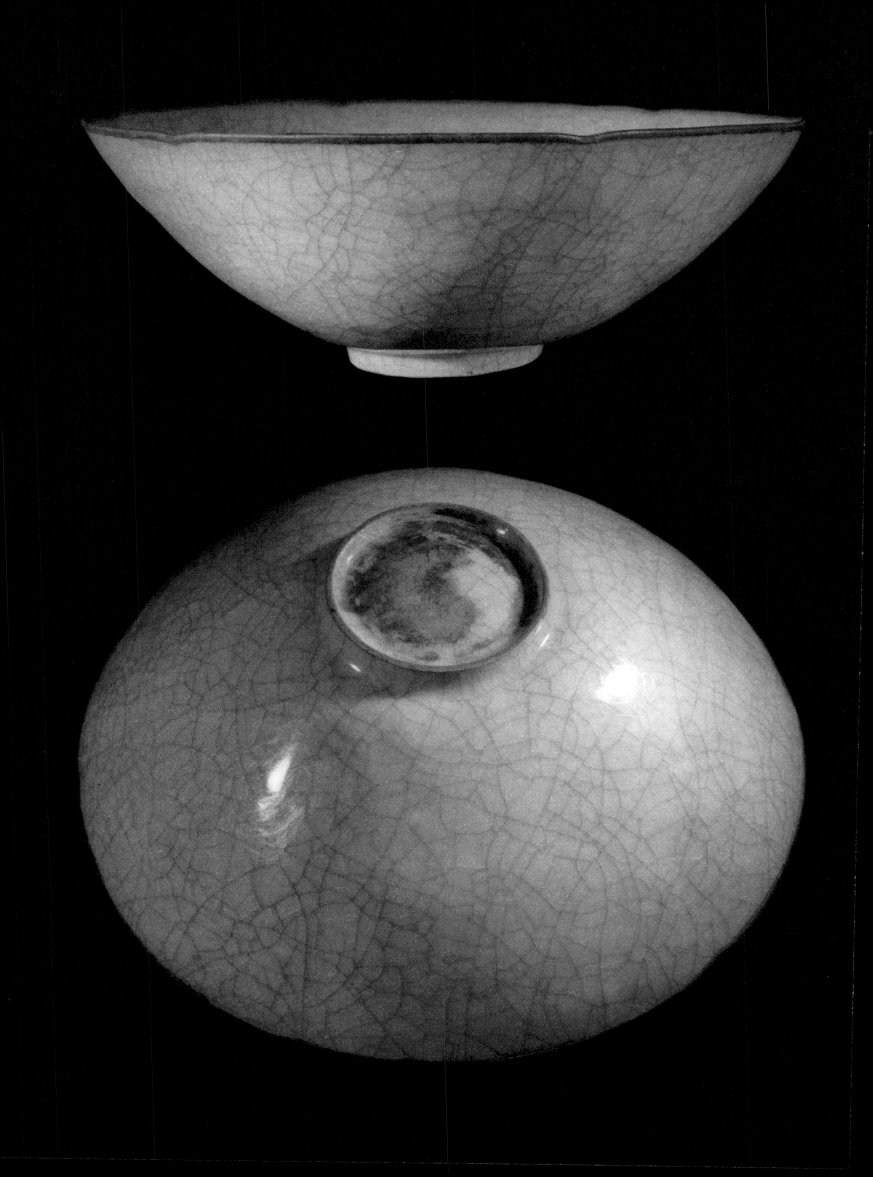

48. CHIAO-T'AN (SUBURBAN ALTAR) KILN CELADON BOWL

Height, 3 11/16 in. Diameter, 10 1/16 in. National Museum, Tokyo

This bowl is in the shape of an open five-petaled flower with five shallow indentations on the rim, which is protected by a fine copper band. It is very thinly potted of a dark-brown ferruginous clay, and a thick glossy glaze, in places thicker than the body itself, covers both the interior and the exterior. The color of the glaze is a serene bluish-green covered with a double-crackled surface; the smaller crackles, which appear to be of more recent date, may be seen beneath the surface. The appearance and "feel" of the bowl when it is handled give the impression that it is made of cut semiprecious stone rather than of porcelain, and it may be presumed that this is exactly the effect which the Chinese potters of the Sung period with their undisguised admiration for the classic jade of antiquity were always striving to obtain. Until fairly recently, celadon ware of this type and quality was designated "Ko Yao" and was thought to have been made in and around Lung-ch'üan hsien, but recent studies have shown that it was produced at the Chiao-t'an (Suburban Altar) kilns located at the west foot of Wu-kuei-shan, about two and one-half miles south of Hangchow in Chekiang. The Chiao-t'an yao seems to have been an official factory devoted to the manufacture of ceramic wares for the Southern Sung Imperial court, and products of this kiln, reserved for official use, were seldom acquired by ordinary people, so that very few of them appear to have left China.

The bowl shown here is registered in Japan as an Important Cultural Property.

49. LUNG-CH'ÜAN CELADON VASE WITH IRON-BROWN SPOTS

Height, 10 13/16 in.   Diameter, 5 13/16 in.   Private Collection

The vase illustrated, which is registered as a National Treasure in Japan, is one of the finest known examples of Lung-ch'üan spotted celadon (known to the Japanese as *tobi seiji*). It has a pear-shaped form with a trumpet-like mouth, and the body is the usual Lung-ch'üan type of gray porcelaneous stoneware. The glaze is of an intense green color ornamented with spots of dark-brown ferruginous glaze, five inside the mouth, thirteen on the body, and three on the outside edge of the foot, all spaced out more or less evenly. Judging from the shape, the glaze color, and the somewhat pretentious decoration, this vase probably dates from the end of the Sung or the early part of the Yüan dynasty.

Spotted celadon wares of this sort were perhaps not very highly regarded by contemporary Chinese connoisseurs of ceramics, for very few seem to have been produced. Apart from a small number of vases of this kind, a few covered boxes and two or three pouring bowls are known to exist in Japan.

50. CHIEN WARE "OIL-SPOT" *TEMMOKU* BOWL

Diameter, 7 11/16 in. Seikado Foundation (former Iwasaki Collection), Tokyo

This rare "oil-spot" *temmoku* bowl is remarkable for its large size and for the quality and pristine condition of the glaze. There is a similar bowl in the Freer Gallery in Washington, but no others are known. These bowls, like the "yao pien" *temmoku* bowls (see plate 33), are considered to have been made at Chien yao in Fukien, but they were extensively copied in other parts of China, notably in Honan Province at places still not certainly located. The copies, however, are for the most part made with a whitish clay body; a coating of brown or black slip on the foot which occurs frequently suggests a conscious imitation of the Chien wares. The bowl illustrated here has the typical weighty, ferruginous, dark-brown body associated with Chien ware, and the inside and outside surfaces are thickly covered with an intense black *temmoku* glaze which stops just short of the foot. The glaze surface is dotted over-all with silvery iridescent spots which in certain light conditions look just like drops of oil floating on water—hence the name "oil-spot" *temmoku*. As in the case of the "yao pien" bowls, this pleasing effect appears to be an unpremeditated result of transmutation during the course of firing.

CERAMIC PRODUCTION IN CHINA
DURING THE YÜAN, MING, AND CH'ING PERIODS

THE YUAN PERIOD (1280–1368)

FOLLOWING the final collapse of the Sung dynasty in 1280, China came under the rule of the Mongols, and the exquisite Sung culture which had flourished in China for the best part of three hundred years was rudely swept aside and replaced by the coarse, robust culture of the Mongol conquerors. It was a time of political turbulence and sweeping social reforms, which is abundantly reflected in the stylistic changes to be seen in Chinese ceramics of the Yüan period.

The famous pottery centers of Tz'ū-Chou, Ching-tê-chên, and Lung-ch'üan, among others, continued to operate after the change of the ruling dynasty, but the Mongolian administrators naturally took small interest in the production of pottery and porcelain, at least in the early years of their rule, and it is not surprising that, lacking official encouragement, the industry as a whole declined, so that the celadon wares of Lung-ch'üan, the white porcelains of Ching-tê-chên, and the Tz'ū-Chou pottery manufactured during this period all show a marked deterioration of glaze, form, and technique as compared with their counterparts of the Sung period. On the other hand, with the establishment by the Mongols of what G. F. Hudson has called the "Pax Tatarica" throughout the whole area of Central Asia from the China Sea to the Urals and extending southward to the shores of the Indian Ocean and the Persian Gulf, routes were reopened to the West and trade moved freely in both directions. In this way new ideas and techniques were imported into China, and from Persia in particular came innovations in the decoration and glazing of pottery which had a significant influence on the subsequent development of Chinese ceramics. A new low-fired glaze of a bright turquoise color which appeared at about this time and was used on Tz'ū Chou-type wares is thought to have reached China from Persia. It seems to have enjoyed immense popularity among the Chinese, and many of the roofs of palaces, shrines, and temples of the time were refurbished with new tiles of this gay hue. But the greatest ceramic achievement of the Yüan period was undoubtedly the development at Ching-tê-chên of the famed blue-and-white porcelain which was destined to become by far the most important of all Chinese ceramic products in terms of the variety and quantity in which it was manufactured throughout the succeeding six hundred years. It has long been an accepted tradition in China that the technique of decorating in cobalt blue on a white porcelaneous body under a transparent glaze was invented during the Sung dynasty.

However, no authentic specimen of Sung blue-and-white has been discovered to date, and even assuming that the idea originated in Sung times, there can be little doubt that the technique was brought to perfection by potters of the Yüan period, as recent researches have shown. A fine blue-and-white vase in the Percival David Foundation in London, superbly decorated under the glaze with a design of dragons and phoenixes, bears a year mark which equates to 1351, and a small number of other specimens are known which can be precisely dated to the Yüan period. In addition, blue-and-white fragments have been discovered at known Yüan dynasty kiln sites in Ching-tê-chên. The researches of Mr. John Pope have also established a Yüan date for a substantial number of blue-and-white porcelain wares in the collection of the Topkapu Sarayi museum at Istanbul and among the assemblage of wares from the Ardebil Shrine now housed at the National Museum at Teheran. In Japan there exist about ten pieces which, based on a comparison with all these findings, can confidently be dated to the fourteenth century (plates 51, 59, and 60) and there are no doubt many other examples in private collections in Europe and America. The surviving examples of Yüan blue-and-white wares all manifest fine workmanship and were evidently made with great care. The tone of the cobalt blue seen through the smooth, bluish-tinged, transparent mat glaze is serene and calm. The designs are grand in concept and painted with swiftly-drawn sweeping lines; sometimes the main part of the decoration is emphasized by means of shallow engraving in sharp knife work under the pigment. All in all, the Yüan blue-and-white wares which have come down to us are masterpieces of technique with a majestic grandeur never quite achieved in the later blue-and-white porcelains of Ming and Ch'ing.

The Ching-tê-chên kilns during the Yüan dynasty also succeeded in making porcelain wares with decoration in underglaze red (yu-li-hung) obtained from copper oxide. The idea was perhaps inspired by the purple or crimson splashes of reduced copper (known in Japan as shinsha), on the Sung Chün ware. However, the control of this red color in the kiln evidently presented great technical difficulties and there seems to have been a high proportion of failures. At any rate, surviving examples of this type of ware are relatively few, although about six or eight pieces are included in Japanese collections (plate 52).

Another Ching-tê-chên ware of the Yüan period, which is mentioned in the Ko-ku Yao-lun (1387) as being for official use, is the shu-fu (Privy Council) bluish-white porcelain, so called because it is often marked with those two characters among foliage in relief decoration on the inside of the dish or bowl. This shu-fu ware differs from the finely potted and thinly glazed ying ch'ing porcelain in that the body is somewhat heavier and the glaze is much thicker and opaque; occasionally pieces are seen with traces of underglaze blue. The English scholar Brankston reported that he found fragments of typical shu-fu ware at Hu-tien south of Ching-tê-chên, and this presumably was the district in which it was made.

The kilns of Lung-ch'üan in Chekiang province, which in Sung times turned out the beautiful bluish-green celadon wares known to the Japanese as *Kinuta* (mallet), from the shape of a famous vase of that type which was taken to Japan some time in the thirteenth or fourteenth century and has since been preserved in the Bishamon-dō temple in Kyoto, continued to make celadon wares in large numbers throughout the Yüan period. A large part of their output was exported to neighboring countries in Southeast Asia and even much farther afield to the countries of the Near East. The quality of much of this export celadon is markedly inferior to the fine Sung wares, but the Lung-ch'üan factories in Yüan times could still produce ceramics of great merit, as is demonstrated by a fine vase in the Percival David Foundation with peony decoration in applied relief, which bears a date mark equivalent to 1327.

In the north of China, the Tz'ū Chou kilns, famous since early Sung times, continued in operation, although their products showed a marked decline compared with the wares of earlier periods. Some of the Yüan pieces decorated with designs in black under a low-fired bright-turquoise glaze are, however, very pleasing.

THE MING DYNASTY (1368–1644)

The overthrow of the Mongols by Hung Wu, who in 1368 founded a new dynasty named Ming (meaning "clear" or "bright"), marks another new period in ceramic history. After more than a century of foreign domination the country was once again ruled by a native Chinese dynasty, and a forward-looking liberal policy came to replace the Sung classicism which had in a sense been continued by the Mongols. The new ideals were soon evident in pottery as in other arts, and, although there was naturally no clean break with the past, the Ming wares gradually came to take on a character of their own. The styles and fashions of the Sung and Yüan periods fell into disfavor and Ching-tê-chên prospered as never before. Many of the other famous Sung pottery centers, and particularly those in the northern provinces, fell into decline and ultimately became extinct. A contributory reason for this state of affairs was the concentration under the Ming of economic and political strength in South China, which caused some of the old kilns of the southern provinces, such as Lung ch'üan, Chien, and Chi chou, to regain much of their former vigor. But by far the greatest revival and expansion took place at Ching-tê-chên, where a new Imperial factory was started by Hung Wu in 1369, after which the town quickly grew to become the ceramic metropolis of China, and, indeed, within the following century, the main supplier of porcelain wares to the world. From this time on, the history of Chinese ceramic manufacture is virtually the history of Ching-tê-chên, and the notes that follow, which attempt to classify very briefly the special characteristics of the wares of the different reigns of the Ming dynasty, are principally concerned with the products of that district.

[119]

The early years of the Ming dynasty

During the reigns of Hung Wu (1368–1398), Chien Wên (1399–1402), and Yung Lo (1403–1424), it is believed that the Ching-tê-chên kilns produced mainly blue-and-white wares and plain white porcelain, but evidently few of them were inscribed with a reign mark, and, consequently, surviving pieces which can reliably be ascribed to this period are very few indeed.

Hsüan Tê (1426–1435)

During the short but peaceful and prosperous reign of the Emperor Hsüan Tê, great quantities of very fine blue-and-white porcelain were made and exported (plates 61 and 62). The Imperial factory was then under the direction of an official named Chang Shan, who, judging from the consistently high quality of the porcelain turned out, must have been a first-class administrator. Painting in the difficult underglaze copper-red was also fully mastered during the Hsüan Tê period (plate 52) and decoration in vitrified colored enamels over the glaze began to be employed with success.

Chêng T'ung (1436–1449), Ching T'ai (1450–1457), and T'ien Shun (1457–1464)

It is curious that no known examples exist of porcelain wares inscribed with reign marks of either Chêng T'ung or Ching T'ai, and only one piece—a small stem cup—is known with a reign mark of T'ien Shun, although it is apparent from ancient records of Ching-tê-chên that the official factory there was not completely out of operation during that thirty-year period. Presumably the official kilns and others continued to turn out blue-and-white porcelain in the Hsüan Tê manner, and this would in part account for the very large quantities of Hsüan Tê-type wares still in existence—quantities which seem to be out of all proportion to the short duration (ten years) of the Hsüan Tê reign.

Ch'êng Hua (1465–1487)

After the middle of the fifteenth century both the blue-and-white and underglaze-red wares of Ching-tê-chên began to decline in vigor. In the Ch'êng Hua era, for example, the blue is thinner, lighter, and "weaker," lacking the impressive depth characteristic of Hsüan Tê wares. Nevertheless the porcelain products of this period are generally elegant in form and finely potted, and the underglaze decoration is free and sensitive. The potters of the Ch'êng Hua period also made further strides in the technique of overglaze enamel decoration, and some of the finest polychrome wares were made at this time, which marks the beginning of the manufacture of the famed Ming five-color porcelain.

Hung Chih (1488–1505)

The reign of Hung Chih was an unimportant one in Chinese ceramic history, owing, it is said, to the fact that the affairs of the state were in the hands of conscientious administrators who concentrated on building up the national strength and in order to conserve the state treasury placed restrictions on the official kilns which supplied the needs of the court. The Ch'êng Hua styles continued to be made, it is supposed, and a yellow enameled porcelain ware, almost the only innovation for which the period can claim credit, was developed in association with blue painting in a simple impressionistic design of flowers and fruit (plate 67). The same type of drawing was also repeated in other techniques, for example by reserving the design in white on a blue ground or in iron-brown on a white ground. Examples of wares, particularly, large dishes, with this characteristic Hung Chih decoration survive in relatively large numbers. The style was also extensively copied in later times and particularly during the Ching dynasty. At about this time the kilns at Ching-tê-chên began to use domestically-produced blue pigment in place of the cobalt previously imported from the West, and the color of the underglaze-blue designs tends to be darker or grayish in tone.

Chêng Tê (1506–1521)

In the reign of Chêng Tê there was widespread civil disorder, and banditry was rife, especially in Kiangsi Province, so that the Imperial kilns were frequently compelled to suspend production, which probably explains the comparative scarcity of surviving Chêng Tê wares. However, a characteristic of the blue-and-white porcelain of this reign is a more masculine style of painting developed from the Hsüan Tê manner, in which writhing dragons and bold lotus scrolls on strong winding stems take the place of the more delicate rendering of the decorative designs of the Ch'êng Hua reign and succeeding periods. The color of the underglaze blue is rather grayish, although it is said that toward the end of the Chêng Tê reign a clear violet-blue pigment known to the Chinese as *hui ch'ing* (Mohammedan blue) began to be imported.

Chia Ching (1522–1566)

During the long and peaceful reign of the Emperor Chia Ching the potteries at Ching-tê-chên flourished exceedingly, and contemporary records indicate that kilns supplying the needs of the court alone numbered no less than fifty-eight, while the population of the town exceeded half a million. The abundant blue-and-white porcelain of this period is of widely varying quality, but the best of it is at least comparable with earlier Ming products. In addition to blue-and-white and three- and five-color enamel wares, which continued to be made throughout the period, the reign of Chia Ching also saw the development of new techniques in enamel decoration, including red on yellow, blue on yellow, green on red, red on green, and, above all, gold leaf applied on a red, green, or yellow background (plates 54 and 69), known in Japan as *kinran-de* (gold brocade style). Many examples of this highly prized ware exist in Japan.

Lung Ch'ing (1567–1572)

The short reign of Lung Ch'ing was a period of financial stringency, which led to a policy of official retrenchment and apparently to the neglect of the Imperial kilns. The wares of the period are consequently very scarce, but judging from surviving examples they follow the Chia Ching style without much variation, though with an increasing loss of character.

Wan Li (1573–1619)

The first half of the Wan Li reign was also a relatively peaceful period, but Ming culture was beginning to decline. The imported cobalt known as *huich'ing* was seldom obtainable, so that a domestically-produced pigment had to be used, and consequently the blue-and-white wares of this period are generally of inferior quality. The five-color enameled wares, on the other hand, reached maturity during the Wan Li reign, and the best of them are magnificent in the concept and execution of the flamboyant design (plate 55). The Ching-tê-chên kilns also turned out during this period a great variety of three-color enameled wares as well as monochromes and some porcelains decorated in underglaze red.

T'ien Ch'i (1621–1627) and Ch'un Chêng (1628–1645)

The decline of national power toward the end of the Ming dynasty affected the Imperial or official kilns, whose products degenerated steadily after about the end of the sixteenth century. However, the products of the private kilns of Ching-tê-chên of this period, a great proportion of which were made for export, are as a rule more lively in drawing and attractive in color than the official wares. They are seldom carefully made and the underglaze blue is often pale and grayish or sooty, but the vigor, lack of restraint, and effective stylization of the painting make them aesthetically more satisfying than many more precise and carefully executed wares. In Japan, pieces of this kind which were imported from China in large quantities around the end of the sixteenth and early part of the seventeenth century are widely favored for the interesting, unconventional quality of the designs. Many of them were actually made to Japanese order for use in the tea ceremony, and they are prized by devotees of the cult to this day (plate 72).

No account of pottery production in China during the Ming dynasty, however brief, would be complete without mention of the ware termed *fa-hua* which was produced at a pottery center in Shansi province. It was a ware with a light reddish-brown pottery body covered with a coating of white slip over which were applied designs in bright enamel colors of purple, blue, white, yellow, green, and black within frames or contours of white slip (plate 66). The contours were no doubt intended to prevent the colors from running into one another, but they were incidentally instrumental in creating a distinctive type of decorative effect. It is commonly considered that the technique of the *fa-hua* pottery was a result of contact between China and the countries of the Near East during the Yüan period.

Another typical Ming ware which must be mentioned is the export porcelain decorated in underglaze blue and colored enamels which was made in Fukien and shipped in vast quantities from the port of Swatow during the early part of the seventeenth century to the neighboring countries of Southeast Asia and to Japan, where it is known as *gosu* porcelain. Surviving examples of this *gosu* ware, which is known in the West as Swatow ware, mostly take the form of large circular dishes, but covered jars are sometimes seen, as well as medium-sized plates and smaller pieces. It is a provincial but pleasant ware with a coarse, heavy, porcelaneous body on which simple designs of flowers and birds, figures, pavilions, and other motifs are painted, chiefly with red and green, in rough brushwork (plate 71). All the pieces have a rude strength and are far from elaborate or refined, but they are greatly appreciated by Japanese connoisseurs for their artless charm. The best collection of this type of ware to be seen anywhere is perhaps the one in the Princessehof Museum at Leeuwarden in the Netherlands.

The foregoing is an outline of the principal ceramic products associated with the Ming period, but in addition, the Lung-ch'üan kilns in Chekiang province, and the Tz'ŭ Chou yao in Hopei, which continued in operation throughout the greater part of the Ming dynasty, turned out some noteworthy pottery. In particular, some of the Lung-ch'üan celadon of the fourteenth and the early fifteenth century is of great merit. It was sent to the Malay peninsula and islands, to India, Persia, and Egypt, to East Africa, and probably also to Asia Minor, as well as to Japan, where relatively large quantities of the ware are preserved in excellent condition.

THE CH'ING DYNASTY (1644–1912)

With the fall of the Ming dynasty, the whole of China came once more under foreign rule—this time that of the Manchu Tartars, who established the Ch'ing dynasty. The early years of the dynasty were marked by revolts, and a state of turmoil prevailed throughout the land. The Imperial porcelain factory virtually ceased to exist, and in the course of the rebellion of Wu San-kuei, which began in 1675, the town of Ching-tê-chên was plundered and all but destroyed. Under the heroic Emperor K'ang Hsi (1662–1722), however, the country was unified, and in the succeeding years the national prestige of China reached the highest level ever attained in her history. With the restoration of political and financial stability, the nation settled down to a period of peace and prosperity which engendered a marked expansion in the arts and sciences, including industrial arts and particularly porcelain manufacture. In the year 1681 the Imperial factory at Ching-tê-chên was rebuilt, and the subsequent revival of porcelain-making began a period which was for long regarded in many quarters as the greatest in the history of the art, and which in sheer technical achievement certainly surpassed all others. But while the Ch'ing dynasty wares are perfect in every detail of workmanship, generally speaking they lack the purity and true artistic feeling of the T'ang and Sung pottery and the vigor of the porcelain products of the Ming dynasty, so that by comparison with all the earlier wares they appear somewhat artificial and shallow.

In the year 1682 the Imperial kilns were placed in charge of Tsang Ying-hsüan, a senior court official and the first of three distinguished men under whose direction the Ching-tê-chên factory flourished and developed a number of new techniques. Tsang Ying-hsüan held the position for eighteen years, during which time were made such well-known products of the Imperial kilns as the fine K'ang Hsi monochromes, including the well-known copper-red *lang yao*, made, it is said, under the direction of one Lang T'ing-chi, a governor of Kiangsi province; polychrome enamel decorated wares in the Ming manner; and wares decorated in colors on a mirror-black enamel base. Figures, designs of flowers and birds, and landscapes were the predominant subjects of the decoration. These paintings were for the most part in the styles of famous contemporary artists; for example, figures in the style of Ch'iu Ying, and flowers and birds in that of Hua Ch'iu-yüeh. Besides the *lang yao*, the K'ang Hsi monochromes include other colors based on copper, which was often fired in a reducing atmosphere to produce greenish or bluish colors such as "apple green," "flame blue," and the enchanting soft red mottled effect with green undertones known as "peach bloom."

The elaborate K'ang Hsi porcelain was followed by the even more delicate wares of the reigns of Yung Chêng (1723–1755) and Ch'ien Lung (1736–1795). Techniques became even further refined and new varieties of highly ornate wares appeared one after another. During the greater part of the reign of Yung Chêng, the director-general of the Imperial factory was Nien Hsi-yao, who was appointed to the post in 1726, but the most famous and gifted potter of the time was T'ang Ying, who became assistant to Nien in 1728 and ultimately succeeded him as director-general in 1736, when the Emperor Ch'ien Lung came to the throne. For twenty years T'ang Ying directed the factory with great success, and it is said that he labored along with his workmen and acquired a profound knowledge of his materials and a mastery of the craft. Under his supervision the Imperial kilns manufactured remarkable copies of Sung wares, as well as polychromes in the K'ang Hsi tradition, and he introduced a number of innovations, amongst which the most notable are perhaps the *fen ts'ai* (powder-colored) wares (plate 73) which eventually replaced the K'ang Hsi five-color porcelains in popular esteem. Unfortunately, the complete technical mastery of the material which was attained at this time led to the imitation in porcelain of all sorts of other substances, including, for example, gold and silver, mother-of-pearl, and bamboo, with the result that, toward the end of the reign of Yung Chêng and during that of Ch'ien Lung, alarmingly artificial and gaudy wares were produced. After T'ang Ying retired from the position of director-general, the process of degeneration continued and eventually led to indulgence in an excessive display of skill at the cost of the essential principles of art. The reign of Ch'ien Lung proved to be the final flowering of Chinese ceramic art (plate 58). In subsequent years it merely became increasingly degenerate and vulgar; no fresh departure was attempted, and the potter's craft with its glorious tradition of thousands of years fell into stagnation.

51. YÜAN PERIOD BLUE-AND-WHITE JAR WITH DESIGN

OF PINES, BAMBOO, AND PLUM TREE

Height, 9 5/16 in. Diameter, 8 3/4 in. Private Collection

At one time it was believed that the famous Chinese blue-and-white wares were originated during the Sung dynasty, but it is now generally accepted that the manufacture of this type of porcelain started sometime in the Yüan period (1280–1368). Recent years have seen remarkable progress in the study of early blue-and-white and the Yüan period wares in particular have come to be widely appreciated.

The greatest collections of Yüan period blue-and-white are those in the Topkapu Sarayi museum at Istanbul, formerly the collection of the Turkish Sultan, where there are reported to be no less than thirty-one pieces of fine-quality fourteenth-century blue-and-white wares, and the assemblage from the Ardebil Shrine housed in the Teheran Museum which boasts thirty-two pieces of outstanding quality. Besides these, there are a number of fine examples in America and England and other examples in Japan, amounting to an over-all total of more than a hundred. Of the several good pieces which exist in Japan, the jar with pine, bamboo, and plum decoration illustrated here is generally acknowledged as the best. The brushwork has the strength and certainty associated with Yüan ink painting and the style of the fourteenth century is well displayed in the drawing of the wave crests on the neck and the arabesques round the top of the jar.

52. MING STEM CUP WITH FISH DECORATION

IN UNDERGLAZE RED (HSÜAN TÊ PERIOD)

Height, 4 5/8 in. Diameter, 4 5/16 in. Yamato Bunka-kan Museum, Nara

The Hsüan Tê reign (1426–1435) of the Ming Dynasty is considered by many authorities to be the best period of blue-and-white and underglaze-red decorated wares. In this piece the combination of the hard white porcelain, the utterly simple form, and the cool smooth glaze surface achieves an effect of great beauty which is dramatically enhanced by the ruby-red splashes of underglaze copper representing the fish. On the inside of the cup the Hsüan Tê reign mark is beautifully inscribed in firm clear characters in underglaze blue.

[128]

53. MING COVERED JAR DECORATED IN OVERGLAZE-ENAMEL
COLORS WITH DESIGN OF LIONS AND ARABESQUES

Height, 15 5/8 in. Private Collection

Colored decorated wares of the type illustrated here were made at Ching-tê-chên
in the middle part of the Ming dynasty and in particular during the reigns of
Hung Chih (1488–1505), Chêng Tê (1506-1521), and Chia Ching (1522–1566). They
were not products of the Imperial factory and appear to have been made for general
sale and for export. There are a number of pieces in Japan which have been handed
down for centuries and recently examples have been found at various places in
Southeast Asia, in particular in Bali, where a number of bowls and large plates
have come to light.

   The jar of the illustration, which may be considered to date from the middle
of the Ming period, is remarkable for its large size and also because it is complete
with its cover. The body is hard white porcelain covered with a thick, transparent
glaze over which the intricate design is applied in rich red and green enamels. The
base is flat and unglazed. Altogether this jar is outstanding among several of the
same type which are preserved in Japan.

54. MING "HSIEN-CHAN-P'ING" EWER WITH GILDED OPEN-WORK DESIGN OF CRANES AND PEONIES (CHIA CHING PERIOD)

Height, 9 5/16 in. Private Collection

The reign of Chia Ching (1522–1566) was a period of great activity and artistic achievement in ceramics, and a number of new techniques of enameled decoration were perfected. These included, besides the well-known five-color or *Wu-tsai,* such innovations as red enamel on a yellow ground, green on red, and green on yellow; but the greatest triumph was perhaps the application of gilt decoration on a red, green, or yellow enamel base. Gilded wares of this type, which include vases, bowls, and plates, have always been highly prized by Japanese collectors, to whom they are known as *kinran-de* (gilt brocade style). Many pieces exist which have been handed down in Japan for several generations, but the most sought after are the so-called Hsien-chan-p'ing ewers, of which the example illustrated here is perhaps the finest in existence. The origin of the term "Hsien-chan-p'ing" is unknown but there is a theory that it is derived from Ch'êng-chan-p'ing—a wine vessel.

This ewer, which has a flattened, pear-shaped body and a tall neck with a long graceful spout, is of pure white porcelain covered with transparent glaze. The principal color of the decoration is red enamel, supplemented by yellow, green, and black. The open-work panel in the center is fashioned with an intricate design of a pair of cranes among peonies and is completely gilded on a base of yellow enamel. The whole is in pristine condition and, as may be imagined, the total effect is one of great magnificence. There is no reign mark but there can be little doubt that this piece was made at Ching-tê-chên during the Chia Ching period.

55. MING COVERED BOX WITH DESIGN OF DRAGONS

AND PHOENIX (WAN LI PERIOD)

Height, 5 7/8 in. Diameter, 11 13/16 in. Private Collection

During the Wan Li (1573–1620) period the tradition of colored-enamel decoration established in the Chia Ching period was continued, and colored porcelain wares of great magnificence were turned out in large quantities. Regarded from the viewpoint of its ceramics the Wan Li period may be divided into three distinct phases. During the first phase (1573–1584), when the Emperor was a child and the affairs of state were in the hands of a regent, the country was wisely administered, the state treasury was full, and porcelains of superior quality were produced. The second phase (1585–1595) saw a self-indulgent ruler squandering the resources of the Empire and the treasury depleted by three great civil wars. The consequent financial disruption was reflected in the somewhat coarser quality of porcelains produced by the official kilns. The third phase (1596–1619), during which the financial system collapsed and crime and disorder flourished, was a period when the wares turned out by the official kilns were for the most part slipshod and inferior. However, the covered box illustrated here, which was probably made during the second or even the third phase, is representative of the best of Wan Li five-color decorated wares, which seems to indicate that there was not a complete breakdown of professional standards even at this time. The colors employed are the usual underglaze blue, and red, green, yellow, and black enamels. A six-character Wan Li reign mark is inscribed on the base in underglaze blue.

56. *SHONZUI* BLUE-AND-WHITE WATERPOT IN THE SHAPE

OF A MANDARIN ORANGE

Height, 6 11/16 in. Diameter, 8 13/16 in. Private Collection

Blue-and-white wares of this type, which were made at Ching-tê-chên toward the
end of the Ming dynasty, are known to the Japanese as *Shonzui* wares and are greatly
prized in Japan, especially among devotees of the tea ceremony. The decoration
is in peculiarly Japanese taste and there can be little doubt that they were made
especially to order for export to Japan. The name is derived from that of a tea
master, Gorōdayu-go Shonzui, who, according to legend, is supposed to have visited
China sometime early in the seventeenth century and while there to have worked
with Chinese potters, who made to his order tea-ceremony wares decorated in
underglaze blue. All the known pieces of this type show the characteristics of late
Ming blue-and-white porcelain and some of them are marked in blue under the
glaze "Gorōdayu-go Shonzui."

This one has a wide band on the shoulder with a design of swastikas enclosed
in a diamond-shaped mesh; the swelling sides are boldly decorated with the pine,
bamboo, and plum-tree motif; and on the lid there is a miniature landscape with
trees, an old house, a sailing boat, and a man on a horse. The body is pure white
porcelain, and the base, which is unglazed, bears no mark.

[136]

57. CH'ING DYNASTY FIVE-COLOR BOWL

WITH DESIGN OF SILVERBERRY PLANT (K'ANG HSI PERIOD)

Height, 1 9/16 in. Diameter, 2 9/16 in. Private Collection

The K'ang Hsi period saw the production at Ching-tê-chên of some of the loveliest ceramic wares ever made in China or anywhere else. The quality of the porcelain was incomparably fine and delicate, and the great range of decorative techniques included, besides underglaze blue, "peach bloom," "apple green," "famille noire," "sang de boeuf" (in Chinese *lang yao*), "tea-dust," and "Imperial yellow," as well as the decoration in three-color and five-color enamels popularized in Ming times. The small bowl illustrated here is an unusually fine example of K'ang Hsi five-color enamel porcelain decorated both inside and out with a design of the "gumi" or silverberry plant and a charmingly drawn small bird. The reign mark of K'ang Hsi inscribed on the base in underglaze blue is enclosed in a double ring, implying that the dish is a product of the Imperial porcelain factory.

58. CH'ING DYNASTY KU-YÜEH HSÜAN VASE WITH DESIGN
OF REEDS AND LOTUSES (CH'IEN LUNG PERIOD 1736-1795)

Height, 6 3/4 in. Diameter, 2 1/2 in. Private Collection

The so-called Ku-yüeh Hsüan porcelains are among the most celebrated of the ceramic products of the Ch'ing dynasty, although surviving examples are few in number. They were first made at Ching-tê-chên in the Yung Chêng period but continued to be produced at least until well into the reign of the Emperor Ch'ien Lung. Many explanations have been offered of the name "Ku-yüeh Hsüan," given to this type of ware by the Chinese, but none seems very convincing. The vase illustrated is decorated with a finely executed design of reeds and lotuses. The fine white porcelain and the flawless glaze surface are characteristic of this type of ware. A four-character square Chien Lung reign mark within double squares, one of thick lines and the other thinner, is inscribed on the base in underglaze blue.

59. YÜAN PERIOD BLUE-AND-WHITE JAR
WITH DESIGN OF FISH AMONG WATER PLANTS

Height, 8 9/16 in. National Museum, Tokyo

This large jar, which was acquired by the Tokyo National Museum early in the Meiji period, is thought to have been brought to Japan in the fifteenth century. The drawing is bold but most carefully executed and has a strong fourteenth-century flavor about it. The underglaze-blue color is particularly clear and beautiful and the design of the swimming fish is enhanced by a certain fluidity of the blue pigment, induced no doubt by accident rather than design, through overfiring. From the form, and on general stylistic grounds, it is inferred that the jar was made at Ching-tê-chên sometime toward the end of the Yüan dynasty.

Two other similar "fish jars" are known. One is in the Topkapu Sarayi Museum of Istanbul, and the other belongs to the Brooklyn Art Museum.

[142]

60. YÜAN PERIOD BLUE-AND-WHITE VASE

IN THE SHAPE OF A DOUBLE GOURD

Height, 22 15/16 in. Private Collection

The entire surface of this great vase, which is in the unusual shape of an octagonal double gourd, is decorated with a design of phoenixes, flowering plants, and what the Japanese call *takara-zukushi* (assorted magic treasures) drawn symmetrically in blue under the glaze in flowing, vigorous brushwork.

The color of the blue pigment is particularly rich and beautiful. No doubt it was derived from imported cobalt of good quality, which was easily obtainable from Persia or other countries of the Middle East during the so-called Pax Tatarica which followed the Mongol conquests of the thirteenth century. Two other vases of similar form and style are known. They are both in the collection of the Topkapu Sarayi museum at Istanbul.

[145]

61. EARLY MING BLUE-AND-WHITE DISH
WITH DESIGN OF FISHES AND WATER PLANTS

Diameter, 21 1/16 in. Yamato Bunka-kan Museum, Nara

This fine dish has a central design of two fish swimming among water plants, which is surrounded by a band of intertwined peonies, lotuses, and chrysanthemums executed in the manner characteristic of fourteenth-century blue-and-white wares. The brush work on this dish is effortless and lively and the "shading" of the underglaze blue is particularly noteworthy. The glaze is smooth and rich, and faintly tinged with blue where it runs over the lip of the dish. The unglazed area of the base has a marble-like appearance.

62. EARLY MING BLUE-AND-WHITE DISH

WITH DESIGN OF PINE TREES

Diameter, 24 5/8 in. Private Collection

This deep dish, which has no reign mark, is ascribed on stylistic grounds to the early part of the fifteenth century. It is notable for its great size, the fine quality of the underglaze-blue decoration, and the technical perfection of the potting—a characteristic of the Imperial wares of the reign of Hsüan Tê. The exposed foot exhibits a fine-grained sugary whiteness slightly tinged with pink, adding to the immaculate beauty of the porcelain body.

63. JAR WITH DECORATION IN UNDERGLAZE RED

(LATE YÜAN OR EARLY MING PERIOD)

Height, 20 1/16 in. Private Collection

This remarkable jar with decoration in underglaze-red (Chinese *yu-li-hung*) is said to have come from the tomb of one of the early Ming emperors, which was broken into and despoiled sometime in the 1920s. The red color is derived from copper oxide, which in firing, owing to imperfect technical control of the kiln, has taken on a blackish tinge approaching the effect of iron oxide. On the contours of the design, however, the color is pink in tone. The body is almost pure white porcelain covered with a thick transparent white glaze. The form is stern but majestic, ten-lobed with a flaring mouth and well-defined shoulders, and the entire surface is decorated with elaborate patterns painted in precise brushwork. The style of the design has much in common with the fourteenth-century blue-and-white wares, and it is considered that this jar was probably made at Ching-tê-chên toward the end of the Yüan or early in the Ming period—that is to say, the second half of the fourteenth century. So far as is known, there is no such large *yu-li-hung* jar in any collection in Europe or America.

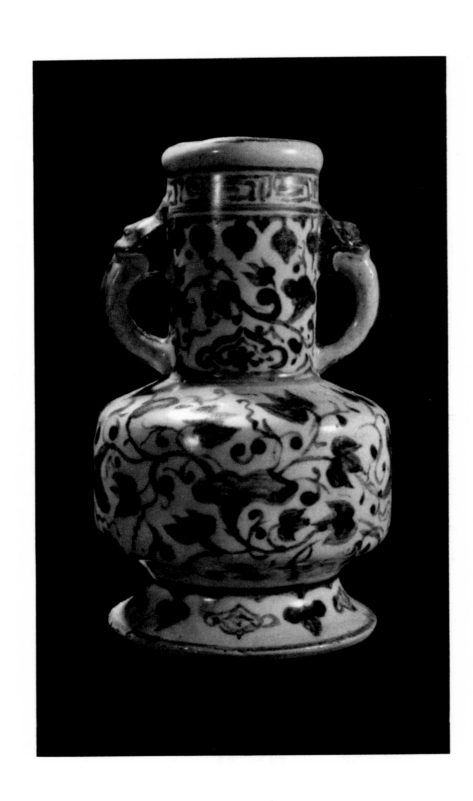

64. EARLY MING BLUE-AND-WHITE VASE

WITH EARS AND DECORATION OF MORNING GLORIES

Height, 5 1/2 in. Private Collection

This delightful little vase was brought to Japan some years ago from Java. It has on the base the single character "Chien," giving rise to the theory that it may have been made in the period of Chien Wên (1399–1402), which, if correct, would make it one of the earliest known Ming blue-and-white pieces. The body is almost pure white porcelain and the design of interlaced morning glories is painted in a strong, deep, almost violet blue under the glaze which by a fortunate chance of firing is beautifully even with a soft mat surface. The tall neck is completed with two ears surmounted by animal heads. In shape and decoration this vase is very reminiscent of the blue-and-white of the Yüan period, and even if we disregard the possibility of a Chien Wên date it seems quite reasonable to regard it as a piece of the very early fifteenth century.

65. MING BLUE-AND-WHITE JAR

WITH DESIGN OF A LOTUS POND (CH'ÊNG HUA PERIOD)

Height, 4 5/16 in. Private Collection

The reign of Ch'êng Hua (1465–1487) is famous for both blue-and-white and enameled wares. The porcelain of this period was very finely made and the underglaze blue was usually paler and softer in tone than in the Hsüan Tê period. The jar illustrated, which is perhaps the best-known example of the rare Ch'êng Hua blue-and-white porcelain in Japan, has a six-character reign mark enclosed in a double circle inscribed on the base under the glaze. The porcelain is almost pure white and crystalline, covered with a transparent glaze faintly tinged with blue. Compared with Imperial wares of the previous Hsüan Tê and the succeeding Chia Ching period, this Ch'êng Hua piece is distinguished by an almost excessive delicacy and refinement.

66. LARGE JAR OF *FA-HUA* TYPE

WITH DESIGN OF BIRDS AND FLOWERS (EARLY MING)

Height, 17 3/8 in. Private Collection

This jar is representative of a large group of Ming wares decorated with so-called "three-colored" (*san ts'ai*) enamels and known generally as *fa-hua* enameled wares. The designs are drawn in raised lines of clay, the original purpose of which was no doubt to keep the different-colored enamels apart, and the over-all effect is not unlike that of cloisonné enameled metal work. The example illustrated is a very handsome piece with the decoration in opaque colors of pale blue, yellow, white, and amber on a full-toned purple-blue ground. It is considered to be datable to the latter half of the fifteenth century.

67. MING PLATE WITH DESIGN OF FLOWERS AND FRUIT

IN IRON GLAZE (HUNG CHIH PERIOD)

Diameter, 7 7/8 in. Private Collection

The reign of Hung Chih (1488–1505) was a relatively unimportant one in Chinese ceramic history and it is recorded that the Imperial kilns at Ching-tê-chên were even closed down for a short time. One feature for which the period was famous, however, was a yellow enamel which was put to a new use in association with blue painting. There are a number of surviving examples of marked dishes painted in blue with the ground filled in with this yellow enamel, and all show a new style of rendering flowers and fruit. This type of ware is called by the Chinese *Chiao hung* or "charming yellow."

The dish illustrated, although of a similar type, is rarer, as it has been treated in a rather different manner. The design of flowers and fruit is applied in an iron-brown glaze on the white biscuit and the whole covered with a transparent white glaze. The dark-brown design stands out sharply against the milk-white background and the over-all effect is one of great strength and originality.

[158]

68. MING VASE OF OCTAGONAL SHAPE

DECORATED IN *KINRAN-DE* STYLE (MID-SIXTEENTH CENTURY)

Height, 15 in. Hakutsuru Museum, Kobe

Like the ewer of plate 54, this fine porcelain vase is decorated in colored enamels
with gilding.   Surrounding the body are eight oblong quatrefoil panels in rich
tomato-red with gilt designs consisting of the Eight Buddhist Emblems and lotus
scrolls. On the shoulder are similar panels, each inscribed with a Chinese ideograph
making up a poem referring to Long Life and Happiness. The lotus scroll just above
the base is very precisely painted in red, green, and yellow enamels. The vase is
known to have been treasured and handed down in Japan for several hundred
years. There is no reign mark, but on general stylistic grounds it is considered to
date from the period of Chia Ching (1522-1566).

A companion piece to this one, now in the Percival David Foundation of
Chinese Art, London, was at one time also in a Japanese collection, and it seems
quite likely that the pair was made, perhaps to special order, for export to Japan.

69. MING *KINRAN-DE* VASE WITH DESIGN OF PHOENIXES AND FLORAL SCROLLS (CHIA CHING PERIOD)

Height, 11 7/16 in. Nezu Art Gallery, Tokyo

This remarkably fine example of the highly prized *kinran-de* (gilt brocade) decoration is one of the few examples known of vases with this type of decoration, which is more usually seen on bowls, dishes, and ewers (see also plate 54). The vase, which is in almost pristine condition (rare in *kinran-de* wares because the gilding tends to rub off rather easily), is notable for its pleasing proportions and for the beautiful quality of the tomato-red enamel. It has no reign mark, but may confidently be ascribed to the Chia Ching period (1522–1566).

70. FISH BOWL OF PORCELAIN WITH *WU-TS'AI* DECORATION

(LUNG CH'ING PERIOD, 1565–1572)

Height, 14 in. Private Collection

Ming decorated porcelains with the reign mark of the Emperor Lung Ch'ing are seldom seen, and the great fish bowl illustrated here is a particularly fine and rare example of the wares of this period. The bold decoration of birds among water plants is beautifully executed in a deep underglaze-blue and brilliant colored enamels of red, green, and yellow. The interior is completely covered with a thick bluish-tinged white glaze, but the base is unglazed. It is technically highly accomplished, and aesthetically satisfying.

71. "SWATOW WARE" LARGE JAR WITH DESIGN OF PEONY

(LATE MING PERIOD)

Height, 9 1/8 in. National Museum, Tokyo

The handsome jar illustrated here represents the class of wares known in Japan as *gosu akae,* and in the West called "Swatow ware" from the fact that they are known to have been exported in large quantities from the port of Swatow in South China to Java and other places in Southeast Asia, as well as to Japan, in the late sixteenth and early seventeenth centuries. The place of manufacture of the Swatow wares has not been precisely determined but it is thought that they were made at a number of provincial kilns in Fukien Province and perhaps in Kwantung. The group includes, besides jars of the kind shown here, large and small dishes and plates, bowls, and small covered boxes.

Although the *gosu akae* wares are coarse and lack the quality and refinement of the porcelains of the Imperial kilns of Ching-tê-chên, the decoration often has a freshness and an unrestrained freedom about it which evidently delighted the old tea masters of Japan, for there are great numbers of these wares preserved in Japanese collections, most of them in a remarkably fine state of preservation, testifying to the care with which they have been treated over the centuries. The jar of this illustration, with its striking design of a peony in full bloom boldly executed in a brilliant red enamel, is a particularly fine example.

72.   LATE MING BLUE-AND-WHITE PLATE WITH DESIGN OF WOMEN

AND CHILDREN PLAYING UNDER A PLUM TREE

Diameter, 8 11/16 in. Private Collection

The plate illustrated represents a type of blue-and-white ware which was imported into Japan in great quantities during the reign of T'ien Ch'i (1621–1627), toward the end of the Ming period when there was a flourishing trade with China, and large numbers of such wares are preserved in Japan to the present day.

Compared with the products of the Imperial kilns this export ware is relatively coarse, but the decoration is usually original and unrestrained and the over-all effect quite delightful. In this plate, the painting of the women and children playing together under a plum tree is executed in strong blue under the glaze and the charming scene is well set off by the border of four broad circular lines firmly drawn around the edge of the plate.

73. SAUCER-DISH DECORATED WITH *YANG-TS'AI* ENAMELS

(CH'IEN LUNG PERIOD, 1736-1795)

Diameter, 5 3/4 in.   Hosokawa Collection, Tokyo

The body of this rare little dish is of exquisite white porcelain with a flawless soft and warm glaze surface. The special feature is, of course, the unusual decoration of the interior, which takes the form of a still-life painting of fruit and vegetables executed in enamel colors of aubergine, light and dark green, yellow and brown.

The term *yang-ts'ai* means literally "foreign colors," and the style of painting on this dish strongly reflects the western influence in Chinese painting which began to show itself from about the middle of the Ch'ing dynasty. The outside of the dish is also unusual. It is covered all over with a bright coral-red glaze on which plum blossoms are painted in gold, providing a pleasing contrast to and a perfect setting for the design of the interior. The base bears in underglaze blue a six-character reign mark of Ch'ien Lung within a double circle.

74. CH'ING DYNASTY DOUBLE VASE WITH COVER,

KU-YUEH HSÜAN PORCELAIN (CH'IEN LUNG PERIOD, 1736–1795)

Height, 8 3/8 in. Hosokawa Collection, Tokyo

This rare vase is another example of the celebrated Ku-yüeh Hsüan ware (see also plate 58). It is of a most unusual form in the shape of two vases joined together and is decorated with a design of soft colors exquisitely painted with shading in the Western manner. Each of the two flattish sides of the vase has a large panel reserved in a frame of floral arabesques and each panel is painted with a different "classical" scene. One shows a youth in the garb of a prince, with three female figures and two children accompanying him, against a background of a marble palace and a three-masted ship with a fluttering sail. The other, which is the side shown here, depicts a young warrior with a spear, offering an apple to three classic beauties. The design is thought to illustrate the story about Paris and the "apple of discord" from Greek mythology.

As is usual with Ku-yüeh Hsüan pieces, this vase has a four-character Ch'ien Lung seal inscribed in formal style within a double square, in underglaze blue on the base.

THE DEVELOPMENT OF JAPANESE CERAMICS
BEFORE 1600 A.D.

MORE than half the territory of Japan is forest land, and for centuries the Japanese have had a plentiful supply of wood which they have used in an infinite variety of ways for domestic purposes. The general use of lacquered wood and bamboo for the food vessels and utensils which in other countries were made of clay probably explains why there was no extensive development of the art of pottery making in Japan until about the end of the Edo period (1615–1867), when ordinary Japanese people came to use pottery and porcelain utensils in their daily life.

The earliest type of Japanese pottery is considered to be that represented by the Jōmon earthen vessels. Examples and shards have been excavated from diluvial strata, which would seem to indicate that they are among the earliest of all known pottery, since pottery artifacts lying in diluvial strata have been discovered elsewhere in the world in only a few areas such as Egypt, the Middle East, and the Mohenjo-daro civilization in Pakistan.

The name "Jōmon," connoting "rope pattern," was given to this type of ware in 1887 because of the characteristic imprint of coiled ropes noted on many excavated pieces; but by no means all the examples have this rope pattern, and indeed there are some with designs produced by a different technique altogether. Jōmon wares were at one time called "Ainu-type earthenware" because they were thought to have been utensils of the Ainu people, but nowadays this explanation has been discarded as mistaken. This kind of pottery has been found throughout the length and breadth of Japan as far north as Hokkaido and as far south as the extreme tip of Kyushu, indicating the extraordinarily wide distribution of the Jōmon culture. The precise genesis of these wares is still not clear, but it is considered that they had their beginnings not later than 2000 B.C. and were extinguished with the rise of the so-called Yayoi culture in about 200 B.C.

The successor to the Jōmon is the pottery of a different type known as Yayoi earthenware. Whereas the Jōmon pots are vestiges of a people who used stone implements and lived by hunting, the Yayoi earthenwares are deemed to be the relics of a society which had learned to fashion metal and had taken to farming for its existence.

The name "Yayoi" was coined by some scholars who observed the excavation of some of this type of ware at Yayoi-machi, in Tokyo, in the year 1885, but since then these wares have been discovered in every part of Japan from the Tōhoku district in the north to Shikoku and Kyushu in the south. Compared with the Jōmon pottery the characteristics of the Yayoi wares are generally a thinner body and greater simplicity of decoration. There are wares of various shapes, including cooking pots, tall vessels for storing food, and—especially numerous—deep bowls.

Yayoi earthenwares were made in a variety of places from about the third century B.C. to the fifth or sixth century A.D., and the style of manufacture, as well as the shapes and decoration, bears different characteristics from place to place.

The Yayoi wares were succeeded in time by the Sueki pottery. The manufacture of Sueki pottery, which starts from the fifth or sixth century A.D., employed new techniques derived from the Asian mainland, and the resultant product differs in a number of respects from the earthenwares of earlier periods. To begin with, all the Jōmon and most of the Yayoi pots were formed by hand and were probably the spare-time production of these hunters and farming people. One can perhaps even imagine that they were individually fashioned by the women in their huts. The Sueki pots, on the other hand, were from the beginning thrown on a potter's wheel and it may be inferred that they were made by professionals who, having selected a site well provided with fuel and suitable clay, took up the art of pottery as a means of livelihood. Another difference was in the firing. Firing of the earlier types of earthenware was by a very primitive method. There was no kiln as such; the clay vessels were piled on top of one another and covered with firewood, which was then set alight. More and more fuel was then thrown on the fire until the vessels were baked. The Sueki pots, however, were fired in a kiln of a sort. The method was to select a small hill rising from flat ground and to dig a tunnel through it near the summit for use as an "oven." By employing this method the heat of the "oven" could be raised very considerably above the temperature at which the wares of earlier periods were fired, and in fact the Sueki pots were fired at about the same high kiln temperature as is used for present-day pottery and porcelain. Sueki wares date from the Kofun time (third to fourth centuries A.D.) and extend over the Nara (710–794 A.D.) and Heian (794–1185 A.D.) periods. They have been found in the north in the area of Ou (Tōhoku) and as far south as Shikoku and the extreme tip of Kyushu. The conclusion that their manufacture was widespread all over Japan is supported by the large number of place names such as Suemura, which even today survive as an indication that Sueki wares were once made in the area.

The number of Sueki kiln sites already discovered is close to two thousand, and they seem to have been established particularly profusely in the areas of Osaka, Toyonaka City, Sado (Kodomari) in Niigata Prefecture, and in Fukui, Aichi, and Gifu Prefectures. Other sites are in Kagawa, Okayama, Yamagata, Saitama, Hiroshima, and Kumamoto.

On some Sueki wares there are traces of glaze which may be both brownish-black or a dark mustard color, and this is known as "natural glaze." It is not deliberately produced by artificial means but is the result of an accident during firing, whereby wood ash from the fire has been blown onto the surface of the red-hot clay and the resultant fusion has caused the formation of a thin glaze.

The oldest true glazed pottery of Japan—that is to say, with a glaze deliberately applied by the potter,—is the three-color glazed ware of the Nara period known as "Nara Sansai" or "Shōsōin Sansai" (plate 83). This type of pottery was fired at a low temperature in imitation of the T'ang three-color wares, and the finest examples are in the Shōsōin at Nara.

In the south storehouse of the Shōsōin there are examples glazed in three colors—green, brownish-yellow, and white—and two-color glazed pieces in green and white, as well as plain green, plain brownish-yellow, and plain white glazed pieces, including a flower vase, a drum, a pagoda, large dishes, and bowls—in all, fifty-seven pieces of different types of this low-fired glazed ware. Apart from being representative of the oldest type of true glazed pottery in Japan, the examples in the Shōsōin are justly famed as the oldest ceramics in the world deliberately handed down to posterity.

It seems that a type of low-fired glazed vessel, tile, and bottle must have been made in considerable quantities from the Nara period (710–794 A.D.) to the early part of the Heian period (794–1185 A.D.). At the present time, known kiln sites are at seven principal centers in the four prefectures of Aichi, Shiga, Kyoto, and Osaka.

In recent years there have been a number of finds in rapid succession of low-fired glazed pottery remains (and particularly green-glazed shards) in almost every part of Japan, and at present the number of shards assembled amounts to nearly four hundred from roughly eighty different places (plate 75).

The two or three centuries from the middle of the Heian until the early part of the Kamakura period appear to have witnessed a decline in Japanese pottery manufacture. The soft-bodied Nara Sansai wares, which, it may be inferred, were turned out in considerable quantities between the Nara period and the beginning of the Heian, seem to have disappeared and the Sueki kilns which were in flourishing production in every part of Japan from the sixth century until well into the Nara period largely fell into ruin. In place of these there sprang up in the central area (Shizuoka, Aichi, Gifu, Mie, and Shiga Prefectures) a number of kilns which turned out coarse tea bowls and small dishes of a type commonly called *yamajawan*. Also there is a type of Sueki ware, thought to date from the Heian period, which was covered with a wood-ash glaze and crudely painted with a brush. Some of these have been discovered at different places all over Japan. For the most part, however, the pottery kilns of Japan were destroyed and at that time the manufacture of pottery was practically limited to the area now comprising Aichi, Gifu, Fukui, and Okayama, where evidently some kilns continued to flourish (plate 84).

The next stage of ceramic manufacture in Japan came with the introduction by Tōshirō,

[177]

the so-called father of Japanese pottery, of more up-to-date Chinese techniques. Tōshirō, more properly known as Katō Shirōzaemon Kagemasa, went as a Buddhist monk to China in the year 1229 and there learned about the technique of pottery manufacture. After his return to Japan he established a kiln at Owari, near Seto, where he began to turn out pottery wares in the Chinese manner, and all subsequent Japanese ceramics may be said to derive from this. Because of the lack of documentary evidence the truth of this legend remains unsubstantiated, but taking all known facts into consideration there seems no reason to doubt its veracity.

In the area around Seto are the remains of more than two hundred old kilns, of which a certain number certainly can be shown to date from the Kamakura period. Characteristic kiln sites of this period are to be seen at Umagajō, Hyakume, Kamabora, Takane, and Akisaka; and kiln sites dating from the Kamakura period to the Muromachi have been found at Tsubaki, Magoe, Hayashi, Takadoya, and elsewhere. Also, remains of kilns of the Muromachi period are known at Konagaso, Nagaso, Karasudaira, Odoridaira Hinokizawa, Taira, Kasamatsu, and Nagane, among others. Buried in these various kiln sites have been found many shards, some with a particularly lovely glaze of autumn-leaf tint and others with a black *temmoku*-type glaze, demonstrating in each case the special characteristics of the particular kiln. However, there are a number of points of difference between Seto wares of the Kamakura and the Muromachi periods. First of all, among the shards picked up at Seto kiln sites of the Kamakura period, fragments of four-eared pots, *heishi* (religious-offering jars), *jimbin* (ritual wine pourers), and incense burners, as well as other types of utensils used for religious festivals and Buddhist ritual, are very numerous (plate 77), while among the shards found in the Muromachi kiln sites the most numerous types are fragments of various utensils and articles for daily use, as large dishes, tea bowls, saucers, and jugs. Even among these articles the shapes, manner of potting, and the form of the foot show marked differences compared with products of the earlier period. Secondly, while the shards of the Kamakura period are decorated with stamped, engraved, or appliqué decoration, the shards of the Muromachi period are almost all without decoration. Thirdly, one of the characteristics of the wares of the Kamakura period, which results from the over-lavish application of wood ash, is the wrinkled or frizzled appearance of the glaze, and the streaks of thicker glaze running in small rivulets on the surface of the vessels. From the Muromachi period onward, because of the higher feldspathic content, the glazes were usually stabilized, with the result that the vessels are evenly coated. Toward the end of the Kamakura period and extending into the Muromachi, the Seto kilns turned out, in addition to wares glazed with the soft yellow color of autumn leaves, large quantities of pottery with a dark toffee-colored glaze which is called Seto *temmoku*. At about this time there were also kilns in operation at Tokonabe, Shigaraki, Tamba, Bizen, and Echizen, and these, together with Seto, are known collectively as the six ancient kilns of Japan. Tokonabe, which lies about fifteen miles south of Nagoya, is a town situated roughly in the center of the Chita peninsula.

In an area running eighteen miles north and south and three miles east and west from Toko-nabe have been discovered the traces of more than six hundred old kiln sites dating from the Heian period up to the Muromachi. This is by far the greatest concentration of ancient kiln sites in Japan, and it may be inferred that the quantity of pottery produced at Tokonabe during those period must have been far greater than that produced anywhere else in the country (plate 88).

Shigaraki is a mountain village at the extreme southern tip of Shiga prefecture. No kiln sites of the Kamakura period have been discovered there, but vestiges of Muromachi period kilns may be seen at Goinokitoge, Minami-Matsuo, and Kamagatani.

The old kiln sites of Tamba exist in large numbers in Hyōgo Prefecture at Hikami-gun and Taki-gun, and the present-day kilns are actually built on Kamakura and Muromachi sites at Sambontōge near Imatamura Tachigui, Tokodani, Genbeiyama, Tarōsaburō, and Ina-riyama.

Bizen, in Okayama Prefecture, has been turning out a particular type of unglazed pottery from Sueki times up to the present day, and the kilns are spread over a wide area centered on Imbe, near the modern town of Bizen. Kiln sites of the Sueki period may be seen at the vil-lages of Miwa and Tamatsu about six miles to the south, and sites of the Nara period are in the vicinity of Imbe at Daimyōjin and Minamiura-Imbe. The Kamakura sites lie to the northwest of Imbe at the foot of Mount Kumayama, while the Muromachi period kiln sites encircle Imbe, where they are known as the Western, Northern, and Southern kilns.

The Echizen kilns, which also have a long tradition going right back to the Sueki period, are spread in the area of Oda, some nine miles west of Sabae City in Fukui Prefecture. The Sueki period kiln sites are located at Kamasaka, Kashizu, Sasafu, Funaba, and Ozohara, while sites of the Kamakura period are at Kumadan, Taira, Masutani, Yakiyama, and Ozohara. Muromachi period sites are at Taira, Ōgamaya, and Yamanaka. In addition there are also some sites of the Kamakura period near Nakatsugawa City in Gifu Prefecture.

Of all these kilns, it was only in Seto that wares were made with artificially applied glazes and artistic decoration, and throughout the Kamakura period and up to the early part of the Muromachi the Seto kilns seem have been actively producing pottery for use in Buddhist ceremonial (plate 77) and a variety of other wares (plates 85 and 86). Thus it was that as early as the fourteenth century Seto became the center of pottery manufacture in Japan and the origin of the word *setomono* as a generic term for pottery and porcelain.

During the period of the Civil Wars, in the fifteenth and early sixteenth centuries, the Nobi Plain was the scene of almost continuous fighting and the Seto potters could no longer continue to work in the peaceable fashion which was necessary for their calling. To escape the rigors of war they moved to Mino, about fifteen miles to the north, and there, receiving the protection of the Lord of Toki, they established their kilns anew. The Mino kilns in Gifu

Prefecture at Toki City, Tajimi, and all over Kani-gun, were built by these refugees, and according to legend the founder of the Mino potteries was one Katō Yosobei Kagemitsu, who established a kiln at Kujiri. In the period of Tenshō (1573–1591), so the tale goes, his younger brother Gōrōzaemon Kagetoyo started up a kiln at Ōhira, while one Genjurō Kagenari established his at Ōkaya, and Iyeimon Kagesada another at Mashizume. Afterward, it is said, a son of Kagemitsu, named Shirōzaemon Kagenobu, began the manufacture of Oribe ware at his father's place in Kujiri; the fifth son of Kagetoyo, named Tarōzaemon Kagetoshi, founded a kiln at Ōtomi, and a sixth son, Jūeimon Kageshige, the Kasahara kiln. In the second year of Genwa (1616), Yoeimon Kageichi established a kiln at Takada. The various wares of Shino (plates 79, 80, 89, and 90), Kiseto ("yellow Seto") (plate 92), Setoguro (black Seto), and Oribe (plates 93, 94, and 95), which were first made at that time in the Mino potteries, were something entirely new with a special Japanese flavor, representing a complete departure from past tradition. In short, during the sixteenth and early seventeenth centuries, the pottery of the Mino kilns broke away from the dull austerity and astringent monotones of the Muromachi period and became bright and free and enhanced by a rich variety of potting.

At about that time the tea ceremony was entering its golden age, and there were in Kyoto many famous tea masters, such as Takeno Jōō, Sen Rikyū, and Furuta Oribe. Accordingly, under their influence the Mino kilns produced, in the main, utensils for the tea ceremony. Nearly forty kiln sites of the period have been discovered scattered throughout Mino, among them Ōkaya, Ōhira, and Takane, where high-class wares of Kiseto, Shino, and Setoguro were made. In particular the Kiseto ("yellow Seto"), produced at Ōkaya-kamashita, and the Shino and Setokuro wares of Ōkaya-mutabora were of very superior quality. Takane, situated on the top of a hill about six hundred and fifty feet high, is known as the kiln which produced red Shino ware (plate 80). Oribe ware was also made at Seidaiyū, at Ōhira, Yashichida, Ōkaya, Gotomaki-yawata, Ōtomi, Hime, Onada, Tsumagi, and Kasahara, but the products of the Kujiri kiln where the famous potter Chikugonokami Kagenobu first started the manufacture of Oribe pottery are considered to be much the finest.

Although Mino is recognized as being the center of pottery manufacture in Japan from the time of the Civil Wars up to the Momoyama period, there were other kilns flourishing this at time at Seto, Shigaraki, Iga, and Bizen, which turned out a variety of tea containers, tea bowls, flower vases, and ewers (plates 81 and 87).

The manufacture of Raku ware, which has rightly been called the essence of Japanese pottery, is said to have started after the middle of the sixteenth century with Chōjirō (1516-1592), the son of an immigrant Korean potter named Ameiya who settled in Kyoto and founded the line which was to last through fourteen generations to the present day. The tea bowls made by the first Chōjirō under the influence of the famous tea master Sen Rikyū are distinguished by their warm texture and soft forms (plate 97). The tradition was continued by succeeding potters of the Raku line and is to be found in the works of such famous masters as Chōjirō's son Jōkei, Dōnyū (also called Nonkō), who was the third of his line (plate 98), and the versatile artist-painter Kōetsu (plate 82). The tea bowls made by these masters have been carefully handed down through the centuries and are highly prized.

75. GREEN-GLAZED JAR (LATE NARA PERIOD)

Height, 6 5/16 in. Diameter, 8 1/16 in. Private Collection

This jar, which in its form and style of glazing shows the marked influence of T'ang pottery, was excavated on the site of an ancient Buddhist temple at Dainichi-machi, Yamashina, near Kyoto. Fragments of a cover belonging to the jar were unearthed at the same time, but unfortunately they have since been lost. The body is of soft light-buff earthenware covered with a fresh green translucent glaze, and the globular form supported by a broad spreading foot conveys an impression of grace and strength. Judging by the style of manufacture and also taking into account the old roof tiles which were excavated with it, this piece is considered to be a funerary urn of the late Nara period (710–794 A.D.). It is registered in Japan as an Important Cultural Property.

76. VASE WITH WOOD-ASH GLAZE

AND DESIGN OF AUTUMN GRASSES (PERHAPS LATE HEIAN PERIOD)

Height, 16 1/8 in. Diameter, 11 5/16 in. Keiō University, Tokyo

This vase with a design of autumn grasses engraved in flowing lines on its sides is of great importance in the history of Japanese ceramic development. When it was excavated near Kawasaki City in Kanagawa Prefecture in April, 1942, it is said to have contained traces of cremation ashes. The ware is a coarse grayish clay burned dark brown all over, and a natural greenish glaze, caused by wood ashes sprinkled on the body during the firing, covers the shoulders and runs in small rivulets down the sides in three or four places. The form of the jar, with an expanding mouth, swelling shoulder, and tapering base, is one which recurs frequently in Japanese ceramics, but the raised band at the base of the neck is unusual. The engraved decoration is also exceptional and rather beautifully done, with a design of melons, Japanese pampas grass (*Miscanthus sinensis*) waving in the wind, leaf patterns, and on the neck a dragonfly. It is thought that this jar, which was evidently intended as a funerary urn, was perhaps made at Tokonabe toward the latter part of the Heian period (794-1185). It was registered as a National Treasure in 1953.

77. VASE OF SETO WARE WITH INCISED DECORATION
OF PEONIES AND FLORAL SPRAYS (KAMAKURA PERIOD)

Height, 9 1/2 in. Private Collection

This lovely vase with its free-flowing engraved decoration under a rather thick, finely crackled, transparent, yellowish glaze of the shade described as withered-leaf color, is a particularly pleasing example of Kamakura Seto ware. Its beauty is enhanced by the broad line of dark-brown glaze which, through an accident of firing, lends emphasis to one side of the vase. The shape, which is referred to in Japanese as *heishi,* occurs rather frequently among Seto wares of the Kamakura period and was evidently a form prescribed for use in Buddhist ceremonial. The body is a hard gray stoneware, and the base is flat and unglazed.

The inspiration for vases of this kind was no doubt provided by Chinese prototypes with similar engraved or stamped decoration under a *ying ch'ing* (shadow blue) glaze, which were made at Ching-tê-chên during the Southern Sung dynasty and seem to have been imported into Japan in fairly large numbers from the early part of the thirteenth century.

78. "OLD SHIGARAKI" JAR

Height, 11 7/16 in. Diameter, 8 1/4 in. Private Collection

Toward the end of the Kamakura period, numerous pottery kilns were in operation at Tokonabe, Shigaraki, Tamba, Bizen, and Echizen, and these, together with Seto, are known collectively as the "six ancient kilns" of Japan. The large jar illustrated is a fine example of Shigaraki ware of the Muromachi period (1392–1573) and was probably made for use as a grain or seed container. It has a body of hard, gray, semiporcelaneous clay, with a rough, pitted surface, characteristic of Shigaraki ware, which has burned red or brown in the firing. The upper part is covered with a natural wood-ash glaze, and there is a simple incised pattern of crosses within parallel lines running around the jar at the shoulder.

Old Shigaraki wares of this sort are valued for their rustic simplicity and complete lack of pretentiousness, and this particular jar is regarded as one of the best of its kind.

79. SHINO WARE TEA BOWL, NAMED "UNOHANAGAKI"

Height, 3 11/16 in.   Diameter, 4 5/8 in.   Private Collection

Shino ware was first made at Mino, about fifteen miles north of Seto, during the Momoyama period (1573–1615), and it seems that it quickly found favor with the old tea masters, for it was produced in large quantities and in a variety of shapes and styles suitable for the tea ceremony from the Momoyama until well into the Edo period (1615–1867). The principal kilns in the Mino district producing this ware during Momoyama and early Edo times were at Ōgaya, Ōhira, Takane, Kujiri, and Ōkawa, and of these the Ōgaya kiln was perhaps the best. The tea bowl illustrated, which is registered as an Important Cultural Property, is regarded as one of the finest Shino tea bowls in Japan and is thought to have been made at the Ōgaya kiln. It is potted of soft coarse clay covered with a thick milk-white glaze. Where the glaze is thinner, for example on the mouth rim, the clay is seen to have burned pinkishbrown. The shape of the bowl is slightly distorted to give the effect of a handmodeled article, although in fact it was thrown on a wheel. A design of crisscross lines (which cannot be seen in the illustration, as it is on the reverse side), painted in bold brush strokes under the glaze, is slightly tinged with pink, and the name of the bowl, "Unohanagaki" (*Deutzia crenata,* flower fence), probably derives from this decoration.

80. RED SHINO WARE STRAIGHT-SIDED DISH

WITH FLORAL DESIGN

Height, 1 7/8 in. Diameter, 6 9/16 in. Private Collection

Nowadays the different types of Shino ware are usually separately classified as plain Shino, painted Shino, gray Shino, and red Shino; and the deep dish illustrated here belongs to the last category. Both gray and red Shino were produced by covering the coarse white body with a red clay slip, leaving the decoration in reserve. The whole piece was then glazed and fired. When the milk-white Shino glaze was applied very thickly the color of the finished product turned out to be medium or dark gray, but if the glaze was thin the red color showed through, giving a pink or sometimes reddish-brown effect. Red Shino wares are relatively rare, and it seems that they were made during the Momoyama or the early Edo period at only one kiln—that of Takane, situated on a high hill between Ōhira and Kujiri. This dish, decorated with a charming design of *nadeshiko* flowers (*Dianthus superbus*), is a typical example of the best of the products of the Takane kiln.

[192]

81. IGA-WARE WATER JAR

Height, 8 1/4 in. Diameter, 9 7/16 in. Private Collection

The ceramic factories in Iga Prefecture during the Momoyama period and for some time afterward were devoted to the production of tea-ceremony wares, and these have since come to be highly appreciated by devotees of the cult. In particular, containers which can be used as flower vases are prized, and the jar illustrated is one such piece. As may be seen, the ware is a coarse, heavy pottery, roughly shaped, and covered with a transparent greenish glaze through which the body color shows pink and amber where it has burned in the firing. The kiln cracks and blemishes are in no way regarded as defects by the tea masters but, on the contrary, as valuable contributions to that quality of "naturalness" which they look for in pottery utensils.

82. TEA BOWL OF RAKU WARE BY KŌETSU, KNOWN AS "FUJI-SAN"

Height, 3 ³/₈ in. Diameter, 4 ¹/₂ in. Private Collection

This tea bowl, which is one of the most revered in Japan and is registered as a National Treasure, is attributed to that great artistic genius, Honami Kōetsu (1558–1637), who is said to have learned the art of making Raku ware from Dōnyū (otherwise known as Nonkō).

The tea bowl, which is said to have been named by Kōetsu himself after Mount Fuji, "the peerless mountain," has a very unusual glaze tone, whitish-buff on the upper half and dark gray on the lower, which apparently was not a fortuitous result of firing but was deliberately effected by carbonization. Tradition has it that this bowl was taken by Kōetsu's daughter at her marriage to her husband's family, at their request, in place of a dowry.

83. NARA PERIOD THREE-COLOR GLAZED JAR WITH COVER

Height, 6 5/16 in. Diameter, 7 5/16 in. Private Collection

This covered jar, which is registered as an Important Cultural Property, is one of the very few intact specimens of three-color glazed wares of the Nara period, other than those in the Imperial repository known as the Shōsōin at Nara, where there are no less than fifty-seven pieces of two-color and three-color wares, including bowls, dishes, and a flower vase. The jar was excavated at Taishokkanyama near Ai village in Osaka Prefecture, which traditionally is the burial site of one Fujiwara-no-Kamatari (644–669 A.D.), a high-ranking courtier of the pre-Nara period.

It is a grayish-white ware covered with a thick green, brown, and white low-fired glaze which has decomposed as a result of burial over the centuries so that the colors are now much faded. The decoration of the cover is in better condition than the rest of the pot, however, and gives some idea of how resplendent it must have looked originally. This particular form is found frequently in the early Sueki pottery, and the distinctive curve from the shoulder to the rounded base and the absence of a foot suggest a relatively early date in the Nara period.

So far the site of the kilns which produced the soft two-color and three-color glazed wares in the Nara period has not been identified, but a small number (about thirty all told) of three-color glazed shards have been found at different places in the vicinity of Nara and Kyoto.

84. LARGE JAR OF THE HEIAN PERIOD

Height, 13 1/8 in. Diameter, 10 11/16 in. Private Collection

The two or three centuries from the middle of the Heian (794–1185 A.D.) to the early part of the Kamakura period (1185–1392) appear to have witnessed a decline in Japanese pottery manufacture. Production of the soft-bodied, green-glazed and multicolor-glazed wares, which it may be inferred were turned out in considerable quantities during the Nara period and the beginning of the Heian, seems to have ceased abruptly, and the Sueki kilns, which were in flourishing production in every part of Japan from about the fifth century until well into the Heian period, largely fell into ruin. The reason for this is not known, but it is a fact that pottery articles datable with any degree of reliability to the period from, say, the latter half of the tenth to the beginning of the thirteenth century are remarkably few in number. It is believed, however, that some kilns which turned out a coarse glazed pottery continued in operation in central Japan (Nagoya, Gifu, Aichi, Shiga) and in a number of places on the eastern seaboard. This jar, which was excavated in 1939 at a place near Nakagawa village in Shizuoka Prefecture, may be regarded as a typical example of such ware. It has a body of grayish, semiporcelaneous pottery and is thickly covered with a glassy natural glaze. Although it is a very crude piece of work, it is nevertheless much admired for its pleasing proportions and expression of "naturalness."

85. "OLD SETO" JAR WITH APPLIQUÉ DECORATION

Height, 8 3/4 in. Diameter, 8 7/8 in. Private Collection

This jar, which is notable for its majestic form and vigorous decoration, is one of the finest surviving examples of the pottery produced by the Seto kilns during the Kamakura period. It is a coarse, hard, grayish, porcelaneous ware covered with a finely crackled, rich glaze of a hue which is difficult to describe but which the Japanese call withered-leaf color. The interior is glazed all over in a brownish-black color. The form is sturdy and well proportioned, and the appliqué decoration of *tomoe* (double commas in the shape of circles) enclosed within horizontal bands of clay and fifteen vertical ribs is pleasingly original. Judging from the excellent state of preservation of the glaze, this jar is not an excavated piece, as are most of the known examples of Kamakura period Seto ware, but has perhaps been cherished and handed down from generation to generation. It was registered as an Important Cultural Property in March, 1953.

86. "OLD SETO" LION-DOG

Height, 10 1/16 in.   Private Collection

During the Kamakura and the early Muromachi periods the Seto kilns produced in large numbers various types of *Koma-inu* (Korean lion-dog figures), which were placed as door guardians at shrines or temples. They seem to have been made in pairs, one with mouth open in a roaring attitude and the other, like the model illustrated here, in repose with mouth closed. Several of these figures survive at temples in the Seto district, and one in particular, which is preserved at the Taichō-in monastery in Seto City, is well known and was recently registered as an Important Cultural Property.

The ware is a coarse, grayish, semiporcelaneous pottery covered all over with a transparent greenish-brown glaze with crackled surface. These lion-dogs were also made at Seto during Edo times, but the later versions lack the vigor and force of the originals and the glaze color is usually a clearer green.

87. "OLD BIZEN" JAR

Height, 7 5/8 in. Diameter, 6 5/8 in. Private Collection

The term "Old Bizen" is generally applied to Bizen wares of the Momoyama period such as vases, waterpots, and wine bottles which were produced for the tea ceremony and are greatly esteemed by the devotees of the cult. In fact, however, the manufacture of Bizen pottery goes back long before that time—perhaps to the fourth or fifth century—and there is no lack of surviving examples of the products of Bizen kilns through the ages. The jar illustrated here, which is considered to be of the Kamakura period, is one of the oldest intact pieces to survive. It is perhaps a product of the Kumayama kiln, which was situated at the foot of Mount Kuma, northwest of the town of Imbe. The body is a grayish-brown stoneware which has burned brown and black in the kiln. The top half was originally covered with natural glaze, most of which, however, decomposed during burial and has flaked off. This sort of jar has a special appeal for the tea masters, who admire it for its natural "rocklike" qualities.

88. "OLD TOKONABE" LARGE POT WITH WOOD-ASH GLAZE

Height, 22 1/2 in. Diameter, 22 7/16 in. Tokonabe College (Aichi Prefecture)

Considerable numbers of jars of this type have been excavated from "sutra mounds" of the late Heian to the early Muromachi period (1392–1573), but no other as large as this one has been found. They seem to have been made to contain copies of Buddhist sutras which were buried underground to ensure their transmittal to the next world, and the style and form are somewhat different from those of the funerary urns found in tombs. Tokonabe, about fifteen miles south of Nagoya, is situated roughly in the center of the Chita peninsula in an area which contains the greatest concentration of ancient kiln sites in Japan.

The jar illustrated is of coarse earthenware with a sharply potted neck and mouth. The shoulders are covered with a thick natural wood-ash glaze which in places runs in streaks down the sides, giving an effect of "naturalness" which is very pleasing.

89. GRAY SHINO WARE TEA BOWL

Height, 3 9/16 in. Diameter, 5 5/16 in. Tokonabe College (Aichi Prefecture)

The tea bowl shown here is an example of the plain gray Shino ware which was produced in the Mino district during the Bunroku and Keichō eras (1592–1614). As explained in the note to plate 80, the gray color was achieved by applying the milk-white Shino glaze very thickly over a reddish clay slip.

Among the kilns which, according to tradition, produced the finest Shino wares during the Momoyama period were those of Ōhira, Ōgaya, Takane, and Kujiri in the Mino district, and it is generally considered that this tea bowl is a product of the Ōgaya kiln.

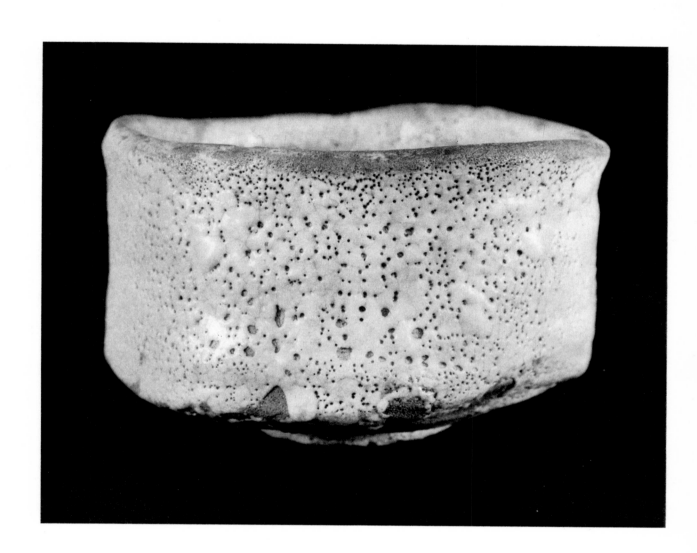

90. SHINO-WARE WATERPOT WITH PAINTED DESIGN OF REEDS

Height, 6 3/4 in. Diameter, 7 3/8 in. Tokonabe College (Aichi Prefecture)

This waterpot is an example of painted decoration on the characteristic white Shino glaze. It is considered to be a product of one of the kilns in the Mino district during the Momoyama period. The body is a coarse, porous, white clay covered with a thick milk-white glaze on which a simple and austere painted design suggesting reeds is applied in iron glaze. This piece is very highly regarded by devotees of the tea ceremony for its nobility of form and the bold, free decoration.

91. BLACK-GLAZED POTTERY TEA BOWL, NAMED "OHARAME"

Height, 3 3/4 in. Diameter, 4 13/16 in. Private Collection

The black Seto wares which were produced during the Momoyama period display the same qualities of simplicity, strength, and restraint associated with other products of the Mino district of the time, such as Shino, yellow Seto, and Oribe wares.

As with Shino, the best of the black Seto wares are considered to be those made at the Ōgaya kiln during the Tensho and Bunroku (1573–1595) eras, and this tea bowl named "Oharame" is perhaps one such piece. It is of a rather coarse gray clay thickly covered both inside and out with a jet-black mat glaze running over the edge of the base but leaving the foot bare.

92. YELLOW SETO LARGE DISH WITH ENGRAVED DECORATION

Height, 2 15/16 in. Diameter, 10 1/16 in. Private Collection

The yellow Seto wares made in the Momoyama period, and subsequently, were a derivation of the brownish glazed pottery which was turned out by the kilns in the Seto district from the Kamakura period onward. This fine dish with foliate rim is covered with a light, transparent, yellowish glaze which has a dull gloss. On the inside of the dish a large radish design is engraved under the glaze, and the decoration is completed by splashes of copper-green (termed *tampan* in Japanese) and iron-brown glaze. The wide foliate rim is also decorated with a simple engraved design of grass and flowers which gives the dish a pleasingly elegant finish. The underside is undecorated.

This piece was probably made in the Mino district some time around the Bunroku era (1592–1595).

93. ORIBE-WARE CANDLESTICK

IN THE SHAPE OF A EUROPEAN FIGURE

Height, 11 15/16 in. Private Collection

Oribe ware was first made at Mino in 1585 to the order of a famous tea master named Furuta Oribe, and subsequently several kilns in the district, notably at Ōgame, Ōhira, and Kujiri, began to turn out wares in the Oribe manner. Most of the Oribe products of the time were tea-ceremony wares, but articles of unconventional shapes and designs are not uncommon, and this candlestick in the form of a European is one such example.

The arrival of Westerners in Japan for the first time in considerable numbers in the last part of the sixteenth and the early part of the seventeenth century naturally aroused the curiosity of the Japanese, and their strange appearance and odd antics were frequently dealt with in painting as well as in the decoration of handicrafts.

The ware is a rough, porous clay of off-white color. The upper half of the figure, together with the jar suspended at the waist, is covered with the copper-green glaze characteristic of Oribe wares, and the lower half has a transparent feldspathic glaze without decoration. The base is flat and unglazed and bears no mark. It seems probable that this piece was made some time during the Keichō era (1596–1614) at Kujiri in Mino Province, but it cannot be determined whether it is a product of the Motoyashiki kiln or of the Kamane kiln located close to it. Both sites have yielded very similar fragments of candlesticks in the form of Europeans.

Although candlesticks of this kind must have been made in considerable numbers during the Momoyama period and shortly afterward, very few seem to have survived—in fact, not more than about half a dozen examples are known. They were, however, copied fairly extensively toward the end of the Edo period, and these replicas, which are generally crudely finished and of inferior workmanship, are occasionally to be seen.

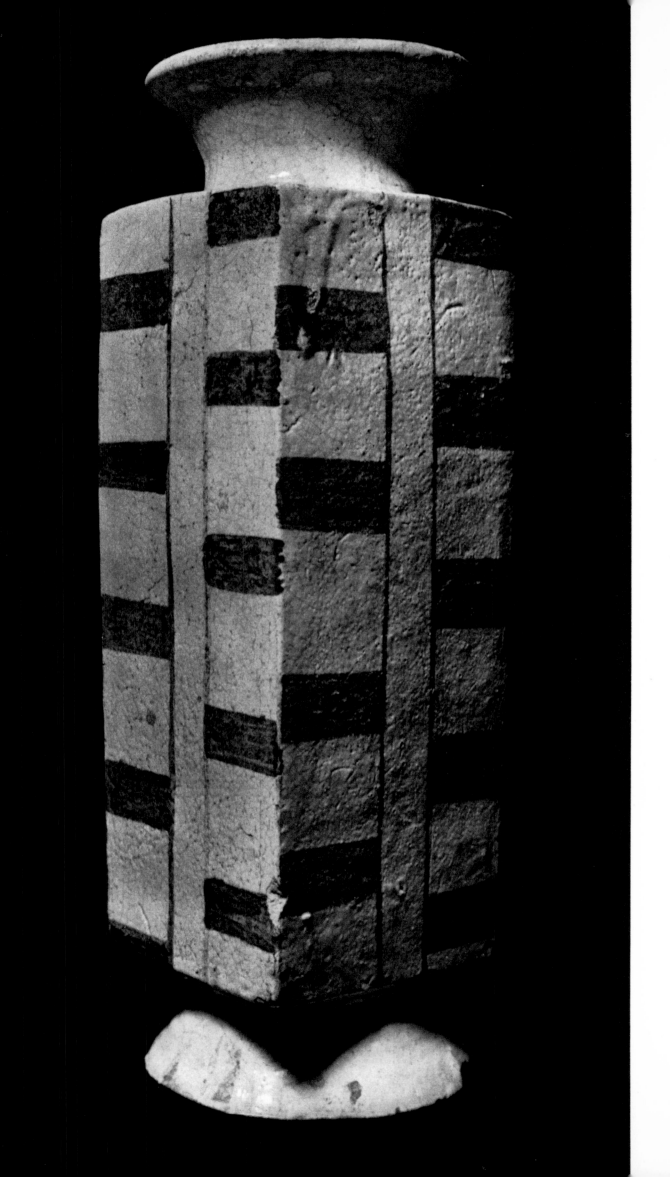

94. ORIBE SQUARE VASE WITH GEOMETRICAL DECORATION

Height, 12 in. Private Collection

The decoration of this vase is clearly inspired by a Sung jade or celadon shape, although in character and feeling it is altogether different from the classical Sung wares. No other example quite like it is known, nor have the excavations at numerous Oribe kiln sites yielded any fragments which might help to identify its place of manufacture. The generally accepted idea that it was possibly made at the Motoyashiki kiln in Mino during the Keichō era (1596–1614) is therefore no more than a guess. The body is a whitish, porous clay thickly covered with a transparent glaze of Shino type, under which the square decorative lozenges are painted in iron glaze which has burned brownish-black.

95. ORIBE FOOTED SQUARE CUPS

Height, 5 1/8 in. Diameter, 2 3/8 in. Private Collection

The several different types of Oribe ware which were made in the Mino area during Momoyama times are classified by the Japanese as: green Oribe, ordinary Oribe, Narumi Oribe, red Oribe, black Oribe, painted Oribe, Shino Oribe, Iga Oribe, and Karatsu Oribe. The six cups illustrated here, which from a set, are exotically decorated in iron glaze with splashes of copper-green, and are examples of the so-called green Oribe group of the early seventeenth century. The body is the usual coarse, porous, off-white pottery, and the form is evidently copied from European glass, which in the early years of the seventeenth century was beginning to be imported into Japan. The intriguing design in underglaze iron defies explanation, but no doubt it is a form of symbolism. It recurs in different patterns on other Oribe wares of the period.

96. FRAGMENTS OF ORIBE WARE

Size of largest shard (upper left), 8 3/8 in. × 7 11/16 in. Private Collection

Shown here are some representative shards from the very large number collected
in recent years on the site of the Momoyama period kilns in the Mino area. They
have been selected to give an idea of the variety and charm of the Oribe decoration.
All are considered to be fragments of pieces of pottery made approximately in the
Keichō era (1596–1614).

[225]

97. BLACK RAKU TEA BOWL BY CHŌJIRŌ

Height, 3 7/16 in. Diameter, 3 11/16 in. Private Collection

"There is no other ware to compare with Raku for tea drinking." So runs an old saying among the devotees of the tea ceremony.

Chōjirō, who was the son of an immigrant Korean potter, started making a new sort of tea bowl and other tea-ceremony wares in the neighborhood of Kyoto some time about 1580. His bowls were sometimes thrown on a wheel but more often pressed by hand and carved and shaped with a flat piece of bamboo. According to legend, he came to the favorable notice of the great tea master Rikyū and through him became known to the Shogun Hideyoshi, who rewarded Chōjirō with a seal for use on his wares, inscribed *raku,* which means "pleasure" or "enjoyment."

Chōjirō made a number of both black and red Raku tea bowls, and those which survive today are cherished by tea masters as priceless treasures. The bowl illustrated, which is known as "Ōguro," is a typical example of his work.

98. BLACK RAKU TEA BOWL BY NONKŌ,

NAMED "CHIDORI" (PLOVER)

Height, 3 1/16 in. Diameter, 4 13/16 in. Fujita Art Gallery, Osaka

Nonkō is another name for Dōnyū, a potter of the third generation of the Raku line, the grandson of the original Chōjirō who is credited with making the first Raku tea bowls. This Nonkō is recorded as having died in 1656 at the age of fifty-eight (although one account says that he was eighty-five at his death).

Nonkō's tea bowls are notable for their precise, thin potting as compared with the cruder wares of his predecessors, and the example shown here is included among the so-called "seven great Nonkō tea bowls."

THE DEVELOPMENT OF JAPANESE CERAMICS

AFTER 1600 A.D.

THE production of articles for the tea ceremony reached its zenith during the Momoyama period, when splendid tea-ceremony wares of beautiful form and potting were made in every district of Japan. Even though the body and the type of glaze might differ from kiln to kiln, the fact that the potting was of the same inspiration was due to the leadership of the great tea masters of the Mino area, many of whom, it is believed, went in person to the kiln sites to fashion bowls and articles in the way they wanted them.

With the increase in popularity of the tea-ceremony wares a number of new kilns sprang up away from the Mino area; these included Etchūseto at Toyama, Shitoro Yaki in Shizuoka Prefecture, Obayashi Yaki in Nagano Prefecture, and Nakatsugawa in Gifu Prefecture. Besides these it seems that there were Takayama in Gifu, Narumi in Aichi, and probably a number of other kilns whose sites have not yet been discovered. All over Japan there was a tremendous upsurge in pottery manufacture, and in particular the period immediately following the end of the Korean wars of the Bunroku (1592–1595) and Keichō (1596–1614) eras saw great developments in the manufacture of Japanese ceramics. Indeed, this period of strife is referred to by some people in Japan as the "pottery wars" because unquestionably the development of pottery and porcelain manufacture was accelerated by the fact that several military leaders who took part in the Bunroku-Keichō military expeditions had kilns built by Korean potters whom they took back to Japan with them. They did this both for their own pleasure and with a view to the general development of the industry of their respective domains. Famous among the pottery centers which owe their origin to these military patrons of ceramic manufacture are those of Takatori Yaki (plate 114), in Fukuoka Prefecture, a kiln built by the potter Hassan for Kuroda Nagamasa; Hirado Yaki in Nagasaki Prefecture, where a kiln was built by the potter Kyokan to the order of Matsuura Chinshin; Agano Yaki in Fukuoka Prefecture, a kiln built by the potter Sonkai to the order of Hosokawa Tadaoki; Satsuma Yaki (plate 112), a kiln built at Chōsa in Udo (Kagoshima Prefecture) by the potter Kinkai to the order of Shimazu Yoshihiro; and Hagi Yaki (plate 113), a kiln built at Fukawa (Matsumoto) in Yamaguchi Prefecture by the brothers Ree Shaku Kō and Ree Kei to the order of Mōri Terumoto.

Besides these Korean craftsmen, others of their compatriots crossed over in large numbers to settle down in many areas of Kyūshu, where they established numerous kilns which turned out wares for everyday use, particularly in the vicinity of Hizen and at Higashi Matsuura and Nishi Matsuura in the area of present-day Saga and Nagasaki Prefectures. The oldest among these are the Karatsu kilns of Hando at Kishidake, Hobashira, Saraya, and Michinaya, and as they were centrally located among the Hizen potteries, all the wares from that district commonly came to be called Karatsu Yaki. The Karatsu kilns produced plain pottery of great simplicity and refined taste in the manner of the Yi dynasty Korean wares. In the beginning their products were mainly jars, pouring vessels, large pots, and dishes—all utensils for daily use—but later, under the influence of the Mino potteries, they began to turn out decorated pieces painted in the style of the Oribe wares as articles for the tea ceremony. Among the products of Karatsu these wares made especially for the tea ceremony have long been highly esteemed (plates 107, 108, and 109). Karatsu wares are classified as "plain" (*mujigaratsu*), "painted" (*egaratsu*), "speckled" (*madaragaratsu*), "Korean style" (*Chōsengaratsu*), "Seto style" (*Setogaratsu*), and "presentation" (*kenjōgaratsu*), while the tea bowls are similarly divided into classes such as *Okugōrai*, *Nenuki*, *Yonebakari*, *Nakaogaratsu*, and *Zekangaratsu*. Almost all these wares can be attributed to the kilns in the Hizen area established by the émigré Koreans after the Bunroku-Keichō wars, and few pieces exist which could be reliably dated prior to that time. The date when the Karatsu potteries were first started is a question that remains undecided. There is a certain tea jar which is inferred by some to be of the Tenshō (1573–1591) era, and one school of thought holds that the kilns were already in existence early in the Muromachi period, but the examples to be seen today are for the greater part datable to the period covered by the Keichō (1596–1614), Genwa (1615–1623), and Kanei (1624–1643) eras.

The manufacture of porcelain in Japan is said to date from the second year of Genwa (1616), when a domiciled Korean potter named Ree San Pei discovered white clay at Izumiyama near Arita in the Hizen district and began to turn out porcelain at a place called Shirakawa Tengudani. Shortly afterward the kilns throughout the Arita district gave up the manufacture of pottery and turned to the production of porcelain. Some of the earliest Hizen porcelain kilns (apart from Shirakawa) were at Hiekoba, Nakataru, Kotaru, Hyakkengama, Itanokawachi, Yamagoya, Maimaitani, Otaru, Nangawara, Maenobori, Nishinobori, Izumiyama, Shirayaki, Tanigama, Iwayagawachi, Yamagoe, Ōdani, Chōkichidani, Kuromuta, Uchida, Komizo, and Mukaibara.

The earliest blue-and-white wares of the Hizen kilns (plates 115 and 116) partake of that rustic simplicity which distinguishes the blue-and-white Korean porcelain of the Yi period. As they were practically all miscellaneous wares for household use, however, the pieces which have survived are extremely few in number.

To continue the story, at about the end of the Kanei era (1624–1643) or the beginning of the Shōhō (1644–1647), Sakaida Kakiemon first began to make porcelain with decoration in colored enamels and so brought new fame to the Hizen potteries (plate 100). There are records which show that the new enameled decorated porcelain of Arita was being exported from the port of Nagasaki to Europe as early as 1646, and by the beginning of the Kanbun era (1661–1672), when all the pottery factories in the Hizen area, following the lead of Arita, were doing a flourishing business in decorated wares, it became apparent that Hizen had displaced Mino as Japan's greatest ceramic-manufacturing center.

The Hizen porcelain was shipped to all parts of Japan mainly through the port of Imari, and many large wholesalers in the porcelain trade lived at that time in Imari. Accordingly, the Hizen porcelain came generally to be called Imari ware, although there were no kilns in Imari itself and the center of production was actually in Arita, some nine miles to the south of Imari.

As the fame of the Hizen porcelain grew, the Nabeshima clan issued strict injunctions to prevent the secrets of its manufacture from leaking beyond their realm. However, they were evidently unsuccessful, as sometime shortly after the middle of the century the manufacture of enameled porcelain wares seems to have been started at Kutani in Kaga Prefecture (plates 102, 103, and 104), and also at Himedani in Hiroshima Prefecture (plate 117). During the Kanbun era (1661–1672) white clay (*petuntse*) of finer quality than that of Izumiyama was discovered on Amakusa island off Higo in Kyushu, and in 1668 porcelain began to be made at the Ōmura clan's kiln of Nagaiyo, while at about the same time porcelain manufacture was being tried out by a priest named Genryūin at Yamamoto in Kagoshima Prefecture. After that, a number of porcelain kilns sprang up: in the second year of Tenwa (1682), Nakano Yaki (Fukuoka); in 1714, Asazuma Yaki (Fukuoka); in the Kyōho period (1716–1735), Nishizara-yama Yaki (Fukuoka); and in the Anei era (1772–1780), Wakimoto Yaki and Hirasa Yaki (both in Kagoshima) and Sue Yaki (Fukuoka). Subsequently, in the third year of Tenmei (1786), a kiln was set up at Miroku in Kagoshima Prefecture; during the Kansei era (1789–1800) porcelain manufacture started at Ōda (Kumamoto) and Shiga Yaki (Tsushima island), and gradually porcelain wares came to be made in almost every district in Kyushu.

Kutani ware is the name given to the enameled porcelain wares made by Gotō Saijirō, a retainer of the Maeda clan, to the order of the Lord Maeda Toshiharu of Kaga, the head of the Daishōji branch of the Maeda family. These porcelains were turned out at Kutani village in Enumagun, Ishikawa Prefecture (about ten miles into the mountains from Yamanaka Hot Springs — the present-day Nishitani village). In those days there was a gold mine at Kutani, and it is said that Saijirō was originally a technician in the mine who tried unsuccessfully to turn out porcelain on his own. After several failures, having obtained the permission of the head of the clan, he betook himself to Hizen, and there, so the story goes, practiced the art of making porcelain decorated with enameled colors. There are several differing opinions as to the date of the establishment of the porcelain industry of Kutani, but the popular view is that it was started some time between 1652 and 1657. In the time of the second clan-head Toshiaki, the Daishōji branch of the Maeda family fell into extreme financial straits, and the kiln is supposed to have ceased production some time in the era of Teikyō (1684–1687) or at latest Genroku (1688–1703). The wares made at Kutani up to this time are commonly known as Ko-Kutani or Old Kutani.

The distinctive features of Ko-Kutani are bold and flowing shapes, daring composition, ravishing colors, and vigorous drawing; and fine examples are prized as representative of the very best of Japanese decorated porcelains (plates 102, 103, and 104).

The Himedani kilns located at Fukayasu-gun Hirose village, about fifteen miles north of Fukuyama City in Hiroshima Prefecture, made not only blue-and-white wares but celadons, ruri blue (lapis lazuli) glazed wares, and enameled porcelain. They appear to have been the work of a potter called Ichiemon, who died in the sixteenth year of Kanbun (1672). The Himedani porcelains are characteristically Japanese with frank, clean designs and fine potting (plate 117).

It was about this time that Nonomura Ninsei first appeared in Kyoto. Ninsei, who may be called the father of Kyōyaki (Kyoto wares), was a craftsman of matchless fame. There were, of course, kilns in operation in Kyoto from the Momoyama period, including those producing Raku wares, and the kilns established by the Shigaraki potters as well as the Fushimi Ningyō (Fushimi Doll) potteries, but it was Ninsei who developed the classical elegance and refinement in enameled decoration which is a characteristic of the Kyōyaki wares (plate 120). Moreover, his style influenced not only the potters of Kyoto but extended to almost every part of Japan. With the rise in prominence of Ninsei, the Kyoto wares enjoyed sudden popularity and a great number of new kilns came into being, among which may be included Old Kiyomizu, Awataguchi, Seikanji, Mizoro, Iwakurayama, Nogami, and Shugakuin; and in the Genroku era (1688–1705), with the appearance of the famous craftsman Kenzan (plates 106 and 121), Kyoto became the undisputed center of pottery-making in Japan.

If we review the principal pottery centers which were operating in Japan during the early part of the Edo period, we have first of all the famous six ancient kilns of Japan which were established in Kamakura and Muromachi times, then the several Mino kilns which became popular after the Nobunaga-Hideyoshi period, followed by the kilns of Etchū Seto, Shidoro, Koito, Nakatsugawa, and Obayashi. In addition, there were the various kilns of Hizen established after the Korean wars; the potteries founded at Agano, Takatori, Hirado, Yatsushiro, Satsuma, and Hagi by domiciled Koreans; and the newly founded kilns of Kutani, Himedani, and Kyōyaki. It is recorded that during the Genwa era (1615–1623) another Hizen kiln was established at Shōdai, and during the Shōhō era (1644–1647) Hongō Yaki was started in Aizu.

During the Shō-ō era (1652–1658) Rakusan Yaki of Izumo, Takamatsu Yaki of Sanuki, and Odo Yaki of Tosa had their beginnings, and the Enpō era (1673–1680) saw the founding of the Osaka kilns of Takahara Yaki and Naniwa Yaki. In the second year of Tenwa (1682) the Koishiwara pottery was established in Fukuoka. Besides all these, other new kilns were those of Akahada Yaki, Zeze Yaki, Asahi Yaki, Akashi Yaki, and Shizuhata Yaki, so that by the second half of the seventeenth century the number of kilns in operation was vastly greater than in the Momoyama period. Subsequently, during the Genroku era (1688–1703), Sōma Yaki was started in Fukushima Prefecture, Iwakuni Yaki in Yamaguchi Prefecture, Utsutsu-gawa Yaki in Nagasaki Prefecture, and Ryūmonji Yaki in Kagoshima Prefecture. The Hoei era (1704–1711) saw the start of Shizutani Yaki in Okayama Prefecture, and during the Shotoku period (1711–1715) the kiln of Hoshino Yaki in Fukuoka Prefecture was established. During the Genbun era (1736–1741) Banko Yaki was started in Mie Prefecture and in the first year of Enkyō (1744) Onda Yaki in Oita Prefecture.

As the years went by yet other kilns were set up as follows: during the Hōreki era (1751–1763), Zenmyōji Yaki in Wakayama Prefecture; during the Meiwa era (1764–1771), Inkyūzan Yaki in Tottori, Isshōchi Yaki in Kumamoto, and Gennai Yaki in Kanagawa; during the Tenmei era (1781–1788), Aya Yaki in Shimane; during the Kansei era (1789–1800), Kosobe Yaki in Osaka, Tokinaka Yaki in Mie, and Kintarō Yaki in Sado; during the Kyōwa era (1801–1803), Izushi Yaki in Kyoto and Sanda Yaki in Hyōgo Prefecture.

Among all these kilns there were naturally some that ceased production within a short time of their establishment and yet others which operated successfully for many years and then fell into decline; but taking Japan as a whole, the total number of kilns active throughout the country at the beginning of the nineteenth century was still quite small. By present-day standards the cost of pottery and porcelain articles was prohibitively high, and there was no question of their being used in the daily life of the general public. The great and sudden increase in the production of wares from the principal kilns such as those of Seto, Mino, Arita, and Kyoto, and the rapid emergence of hundreds or even thousands of small kilns in every area of the country did not come about until after the Bunka-Bunsei eras (1804–1830) toward the end of the Edo period.

99. WATERPOT OF KARATSU WARE

Height, 6 9/16 in. Diameter, 8 1/4 in. Private Collection

Karatsu pottery is divided by Japanese connoisseurs into several categories according to the different kinds of glazing; these include *mujigaratsu* (plain), *egaratsu*
(painted), *madaragaratsu* (speckled), and *Chōsengaratsu* (Korean type). This fine
waterpot is an example of *Chōsengaratsu* and was undoubtedly made especially for
the tea ceremony, as were practically all the other pottery articles of this type comprising in the main tea bowls, vases, basket-shaped dishes with handles, and wine
cups. These wares were turned out in quantities during the Keichō-Genwa
eras (1601–1624) at a number of kilns in Saga Prefecture and particularly at Fuji-
nokawachi, near Imari.   This piece has a body of dark gray ferruginous clay,
and the top half is glazed in a caramel-brown color with a thick white glaze
applied over it which has run down the sides like a waterfall to create a fascina-
ting and beautiful effect of well-balanced irregularity. The form, relatively low
and narrowing slightly toward the flat base, conveys an impression of rocklike
stability.

100. JAR, KAKIEMON TYPE

WITH OVERGLAZE ENAMEL DECORATION

Height, 6 3/8 in.   Diameter, 6 9/16 in.   Private Collection

At about the end of the Kanei era (1624–1643) or shortly afterward, Sakaida
Kizaemon of Nangawata, near Arita, later known as Kakiemon, first began to make
wares decorated with colored enamels after the fashion of the Chinese porcelains
of the late Ming period. These wares achieved immediate popularity and were
turned out in relatively large quantities by succeeding generations of the Kakiemon
family and also, no doubt, by a number of contemporary imitators, so that it is not
now possible to distinguish with any degree of certainty among the surviving pieces
those actually made or decorated by the first Kakiemon. However, the jar illustrated here is certainly one of the older types of Kakiemon ware, as may be judged
from the style and quality of the underglaze-blue decoration on the shoulder,
which is reminiscent of the early Arita blue-and-white wares, and the fact that the
porcelain lacks the refinement and gloss chracteristic of the milk-white Kakiemon
ware of the *nigoshi-de* (translucent type) period when technical perfection had
been achieved. The drawing also is delightfully strong and unrestrained, which
is perhaps indicative of an immature period.

101. LARGE DISH OF NABESHIMA WARE

WITH DESIGN OF HIBISCUS

Diameter, 12 3/8 in. Private Collection

The ceramic factory run by the Nabeshima clan in Saga Prefecture produced porcelain wares reserved for the use of the feudal lords of Nabeshima, who used to send them as official gifts to the Shōgun and to the lords of other fiefs.

The mass of Nabeshima wares, therefore, are food dishes of various sizes with designs which tend to be somewhat formal. For obvious reasons they were usually made in sets of ten or more exactly similar pieces, and the decoration was very precisely applied in underglaze blue and overglaze enamels. The kiln was originally set up near Arita, but some time about the Empō era (1674–1681) it was moved to Ōkōchi, a few miles away, where it continued to turn out fine-quality porcelain which perhaps reached the highest point of technical perfection during the Genroku (1689–1704) and Hōei (1705–1711) eras. This kiln also turned out a small quantity of blue-and-white wares as well as some celadon articles, but its fame rests on the colored Nabeshima porcelain with its unbelievable variety of beautiful designs of great originality and imagination.

The large dish illustrated here, although perhaps of a slightly later date than the best period of Nabeshima ware, is nevertheless a splendid and representative example which has long been famous in Japan. It is registered as an Important Cultural Property.

102. LARGE DISH OF "OLD KUTANI" WARE

WITH DESIGN OF BIRDS AND FLOWERS

Diameter, 16 11/16 in. Private Collection

This dish, which is regarded as one of the finest among the relatively large number of surviving Kutani dishes in Japan, is admired for the vigorous and colorful design, reminiscent of the grandiose, brilliant screen painting of the Momoyama period. The body is of grayish-white porcelain, and the shape became slightly distorted in firing, owing no doubt to some lack of resistance to heat in the quality of the clay available to the early potters of Kutani. The dish is covered with the thick, blue-tinged, white mat glaze characteristic of the early Kutani wares, and the design is painted in strong colors of green, indigo, yellow, red, and black enamels over the glaze. The exterior of the dish is also decorated with a single but powerfully executed design of the three felicitous plants, pine, bamboo, and plum tree. This piece is considered to be a product of the earliest period of the Kutani kiln, which is said to have been established by Gotō Saijirō to the order of the Lord Maeda Toshiharu of Daishōji in the middle of the seventeenth century. It is registered as an Important Cultural Property.

103. SQUARE DISH OF "OLD KUTANI" WARE

Height, 3 1/16 in. Length of side, 9 3/16 in. Private Collection

No other surviving piece of "Old Kutani" ware can boast such an unusual design as this, which has been described as "paths through the paddy-fields." A close examination of the dish reveals that the highly original decoration was a clever device inspired by the need to conceal flaws in the body. The ware is the grayish-white porcelain characteristic of Kutani, pressed into shape in a pottery mold and glazed with the typical opaque-white, dull Kutani glaze. Through some fault in the potting or in the quality of the clay itself the heat of the kiln caused several large cracks in the base; the decorator has covered them up with broadly painted indigo lines and then used these as a basis for his design. The exterior of the dish is undecorated, but the base is covered with an enameled decoration of indigo checks, also designed to cover up the crack. Notwithstanding the unpremeditated rendering of the design on this dish, it is undoubtedly highly successful and achieves a strangely "modern" effect.

104.   DISH OF "OLD KUTANI" WARE

WITH DESIGN OF PEONY AND KINGFISHER

Diameter, 13 13/16 in.   Private Collection

The "Old Kutani" dish illustrated—one of a total of five Kutani pieces which have been designated as Important Cultural Properties—is remarkable for the simple but very powerfully executed design.   The body is of the typical grayish-white Kutani porcelain thickly covered with a milky-white glaze.   The colors used are the characteristic aubergine, yellow, and green of early Kutani wares.

105. INCENSE BURNER IN THE SHAPE OF A PHEASANT, DECORATED WITH OVERGLAZE ENAMELS

Height, 7 1/16 in. Length, 18 3/4 in. Width, 4 3/4 in.
Art Gallery of Ishikawa Prefecture

This incense burner is one of the best-known of the works attributed to Ninsei, one of the most celebrated potters of Japan, who worked at Awata and other districts of Kyoto in the second half of the seventeenth century. He was an accomplished decorator with a mastery of enameling in many colors and in silver and gold as well as the more ordinary painting in brown. Numerous examples of Ninsei's work exist in Japan, including teacups and a number of splendid large *cha-tsubo* (tea caddies with four ears) popularly known by names descriptive of the striking decoration, such as "The Wistaria Jar," "The Young Pines," "The Plum Tree Jar," "Mount Yoshino," and so on. The beautifully modeled pheasant incense burner illustrated is in two parts, consisting of a base and a cover, the latter perforated to permit the incense smoke to rise. The entire surface is covered with a pattern of down and feathers executed in blue, green, and purple enamels, outlined distinctly with black, red, and gold. The body is a fine, grayish-white porcelain. On the inside of the cover and also on the base are stamped the Ninsei mark surmounted by a paired-leaf crest, a mark said to have been used by Ninsei in his later years. According to tradition this piece, which is registered as a National Treasure, was preserved for many years as an heirloom of the Maeda family, the rulers of the Kaga fief, but passed from their possession at the end of the last century and is now in the Art Gallery of Ishikawa Prefecture.

107. KARATSU WARE JAR

Height, 6 13/16 in. Private Collection

As explained in the note accompanying plate 99, Karatsu wares are divided into several categories according to the different types of glaze. This jar, which is perhaps the finest of its kind, is an example of *madaragaratsu* or speckled Karatsu pottery. The body is of the rough, hard, ferruginous clay peculiar to Karatsu wares, and the glaze which covers it is white and translucent, and relatively thinly applied. Splashes of iron-oxide slip are scattered irregularly along the mouth-rim and on the shoulder, and the glaze surface is speckled. The form is an impressive one with a wide mouth, a swelling body, and a large, low foot. It is not possible to say for certain when or in which of the several Karatsu kilns this jar was made, but it probably dates from the end of the sixteenth or the beginning of the seventeenth century.

108. TEA BOWL OF *EGARATSU* WARE WITH IRIS DESIGN

Height, 3 5/8 in. Diameter, 4 13/16 in. Private Collection

The tea bowl with iris design shown here is a typical example of *egaratsu* (painted Karatsu) ware covered with a translucent silica glaze made from ashes of rice straw, and decorated with a dark-brown ferrous glaze. Tea bowls and other tea-ceremony wares of this kind were made in large quantities by a number of kilns in the Hizen district, including especially the potteries of Dōzono, Yakiyama, and Michinaya. This bowl, which has a nearly straight-sided cylindrical form with a slight bulge at the waist, a flat interior bottom, a wide foot, and an unglazed base revealing a grayish body of coarse texture, was probably made at one of the Kishidake kilns during the Momoyama period.

109. TEA CADDY OF KARATSU WARE

WITH PAINTED DESIGN OF A PERSIMMON TREE

Height, 6 7/8 in. Private Collection

This delightful tea container is of the type known as *egaratsu* (painted Karatsu). The beauty of the swelling globular form is enhanced by the three loop-ears which, however, are not purely decorative, but have a functional purpose. They were made so that a cord could be passed through them to secure a lid tightly to the tea caddy and so keep the contents dry.

This piece has the typical ferruginous body characteristic of Karatsu pottery and is covered with a thick, finely crackled, pearly-gray glaze. The simple and effective design of a fruit-bearing persimmon tree which covers the exterior surface is applied with swift impressionistic brush strokes in iron-black glaze. It is generally considered to be a product of the Dōzono kiln of the Momoyama period.

110. FIVE KARATSU POTTERY WINE CUPS

Heights: (a) top right, 2 11/16 in.; (b) top left, 2 1/4 in.; (c) lower right, 2 1/2 in.;

(d) lower center, 2 13/16 in.; (e) lower left, 2 15/16 in. Private Collection

These are five different types of wine cups selected to show some of the many varieties of Karatsu wares made in this form.

The cup in the top right-hand corner of the illustration is an example of *madaragaratsu* (speckled Karatsu) of the Momoyama period. It has a coarse, gray, semiporcelaneous body covered with a transparent straw-ash glaze.

The one in the lower right-hand corner, which is glazed on one side with a smooth transparent straw-ash glaze and on the other with a thick, translucent, brown glaze, is an unusual piece of great charm in *Chōsengaratsu* (Korean) style.

The small cup at the upper left is of a shape known in Japan as *guinomi* (drink in one gulp!) and is an example of *mujigaratsu* (plain Karatsu) of the Momoyama period.

The two others, in the lower center and at the lower left, are *egaratsu* (painted Karatsu) cups and perhaps may be dated a little later than the former three. They were probably made early in the seventeenth century.

111. FRAGMENTS OF *EGARATSU* (PAINTED KARATSU) WARES

Width of largest shard (upper left), 5 7/8 in. Private Collection

The fragments of decorated pottery illustrated here have been selected to give an idea of the great variety of styles of decoration to be found among the *egaratsu* wares. In every case the body is the typical Karatsu hard, gray, semiporcelaneous clay, with a simple, free design painted in iron-oxide black or brown under a transparent straw-ash glaze. All the fragments, which are from kiln sites in the Kishidake area, are thought to date from the first two or three decades of the seventeenth century.

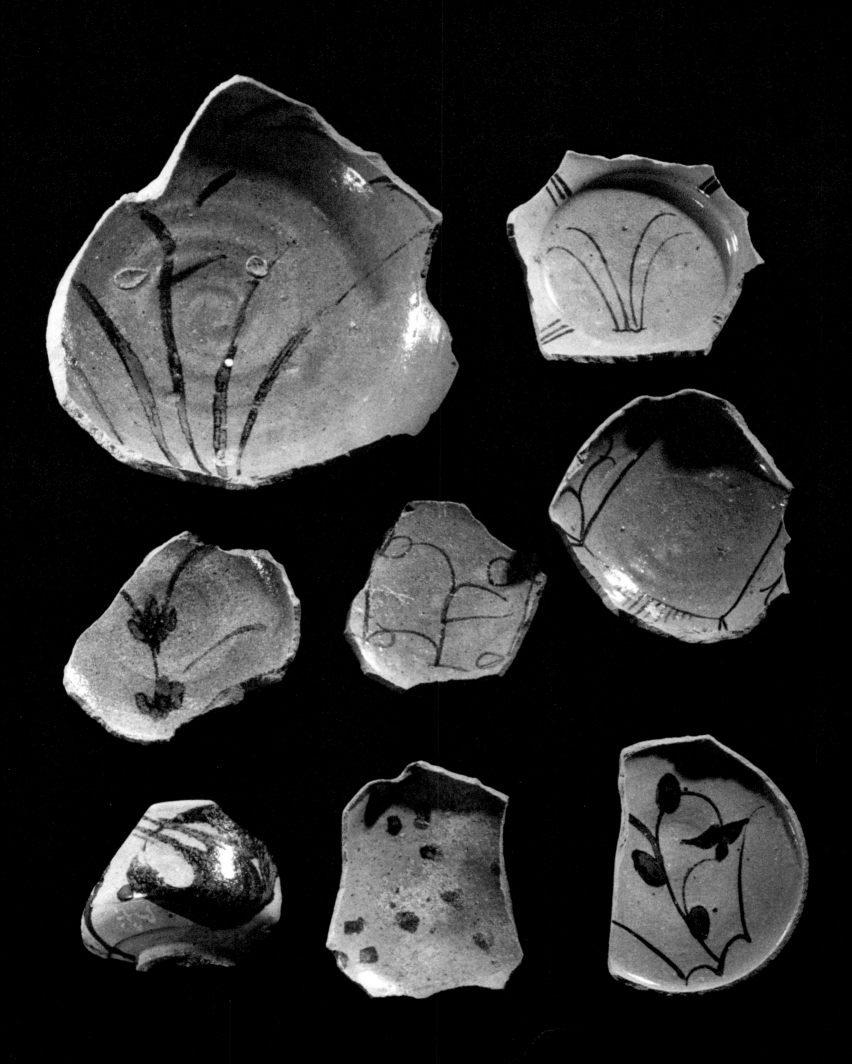

112. "OLD SATSUMA" WATERPOT

Height, 6 5/16 in. Diameter, 7 3/8 in. Private Collection

After the Korean wars of the Bunroku (1592–1595) and Keichō (1596–1614) eras, a number of pottery kilns were established in Japan under the direction of Korean potters who accompanied the military leaders on their return from Korea. Among these was a kiln built at Chōsa in Udo (Kagoshima Prefecture) by a Korean potter named Kinkai to the order of Shimazu Yoshihiro, the Lord of Satsuma. For the most part this kiln produced tea-ceremony ware, in particular tea bowls and small tea caddies, of which considerable numbers survive, but it is seldom that large pieces of Satsuma ware may be seen, and waterpots of the kind illustrated here are very rare. This piece has a body of pliable ferruginous clay and is glazed all over with a thick coating of dark-brown mat glaze. A second layer of opalescent white glaze has been applied to the top rim of the jar and has run down to give the effect of a lustrous black band about an inch and a quarter wide running around the shoulder. The pottery is thin and the piece quite surprisingly light in weight. It has a flat unglazed base.

[263]

113. "OLD HAGI" TEA BOWL, NAMED "HAKUU" (WHITE RAIN)

Height, 4 in. Diameter, 3 7/16 in. Private Collection

There is an old saying among tea-ceremony people in Japan, "First Raku, second Hagi, third Karatsu." However, it is by no means always easy to identify Hagi tea bowls of the earliest period, as the kiln appears to have turned out a great variety of pottery including pieces made in imitation of the Korean *Ido* bowls (plate 144) as well as Oribe and other styles. The Hagi kiln is said to have been built after the Bunroku-Keichō wars by a Korean immigrant potter named Rikei, who worked to the order of the Lord Mōri Terumoto and later adopted the Japanese name of Saka Kōraizaemón. He founded a line of potters who established other kilns in the neighborhood and continued to work in the same manner.

While it is not possible to say with certainty that the Hagi tea bowl illustrated here was made by the original Rikei, it is certainly an example of a very early period, as may be judged from the potting and particularly from the construction of the foot.

The body is of a coarse, porous pottery with a small iron content, and the glaze, which is thickly applied, is opaque white, covered all over with a fine crackle.

114. "OLD TAKATORI" SAKE BOTTLE

Height, 4 in. Diameter, 3 9/16 in. Private Collection

The first Takatori kiln was built in the foothills of a mountain of that name in 1602 by a Korean immigrant potter named Hassan who accompanied the Lord Kuroda Nagamasa on his return from the Korean wars at the end of the sixteenth century. Later the kiln site was moved several times, presumably in a quest for better materials, and was ultimately established at Higashiyama near the modern city of Fukuoka; but the wares turned out continued to be called "Takatori" from their association with Hassan's original venture.

This sake bottle, which was excavated from one of the earlier kiln sites situated near the village of Yamada, may possibly have been made by Hassan himself. It has a coarse grayish-white body thickly covered with an opaque white Hagi-type glaze, and the somewhat clumsy form and misshapen mouth evokes a tender feeling in Japanese devotees of the tea ceremony.

115. HIZEN BLUE-AND-WHITE PLATE WITH DESIGN OF A RABBIT

Diameter 6 3/16 in. Private Collection

The most attractive of Japanese blue-and-white porcelains in the eyes of the tea masters are those primitive pieces which were produced in the Hizen district during the Genna (1616–1624) and Kanei (1625–1643) eras, when the manufacture of porcelain in Japan was in its infancy. This dish with a design of a rabbit and underglaze-blue splashes was excavated from a kiln site at Hiekoba, quite close to Shirakawa Tengudani, where according to tradition the Korean immigrant potter Ree San Pei first began to make true porcelain in Japan. The body is a grayish porcelain with a trace of iron in its composition, and it may be inferred that the underglaze blue, which is rather dark in color, was imported in bulk from China. It is evident that the design also was copied from Chinese blue-and-white wares which at that time were being imported into Japan in large quantities, but the drawing of the rabbit and the general execution of the design have a marked Japanese flavor about them.

116. HIZEN BLUE-AND-WHITE DISH

WITH DESIGN OF FLOWERS AND GRASSES

Diameter, 5 13/16 in. Private Collection

This dish is another example of one of the earliest of the Japanese blue-and-white porcelain wares, and, like the piece illustrated in plate 115, it is a "waster," picked up on the site of an ancient kiln at Hiekoba, near Shirakawa Tengudani (in the modern Arita). The decoration bears witness to the strong influence of the Korean blue-and-white wares of the Yi period on the Japanese porcelain of the time.

117. HIMEDANI YAKI DISH WITH POMEGRANATE DESIGN

IN COLORED ENAMELS

Diameter, 7 3/16 in. Private Collection

The Himedani kiln, which was established early in the Edo period (1615–1867) near the city of Fukuyama in Hiroshima Prefecture, produced porcelain decorated in colored enamels very similar to the contemporary Kutani wares. The kiln is also said to have made blue-and-white wares as well as a type of celadon.

Judging from the surviving wares of this kiln, which unfortunately are few in number, the quality of the porcelain is quite fine and the designs partake of very simple forms such as a single maple leaf, a lone morning-glory, or a sprig of camellias rendered with great feeling.

The dish shown here is decorated with a design of a pomegranate and accompanying foliage in red and green enamels, and it has many of the characteristics of the best-quality Kutani porcelain.

118. SMALL DISH OF NABESHIMA WARE

WITH DESIGN OF PEONIES

Diameter, 4 1/2 in. Private Collection

A wealth of original decorative motifs is to be found among the great variety of
Nabeshima wares (see note to plate 101); the design of peonies enameled on a
background of swirling currents of underglaze blue on this dish is particularly
intriguing and highly successful.

The high foot characteristic of all Nabeshima dishes of this period is in this
case undecorated, though in dishes of a larger size it is more usual to find underglaze-blue decoration all around the foot.

[275]

119. FOUR SHŌDAI YAKI PETAL-SHAPED DISHES

Length of each, 5 ¹/₈ in. Private Collection

Shōdai Yaki, which is another product of the Hizen district of Kyūshu, is in many respects not unlike the Karatsu pottery. It was first made early in the Edo period by a potter from the Tamba district who founded a kiln in the year 1634 in the foothills of Mount Shōdai in Kumamoto Prefecture. Subsequently, a number of other potters were attracted to the district and set up kilns which continued to flourish and to turn out pottery in the tradition of the original Shōdai Yaki until well into the Meiji period (1868–1911).

The four dishes illustrated have no date mark or other indication of origin, but they are thought to date from about the middle of the eighteenth century.

The ware is of a coarse ferruginous clay covered with a coat of opaque straw-ash glaze. In spots where the glaze has run thinly, the body is exposed and has burned to a dark purple color.

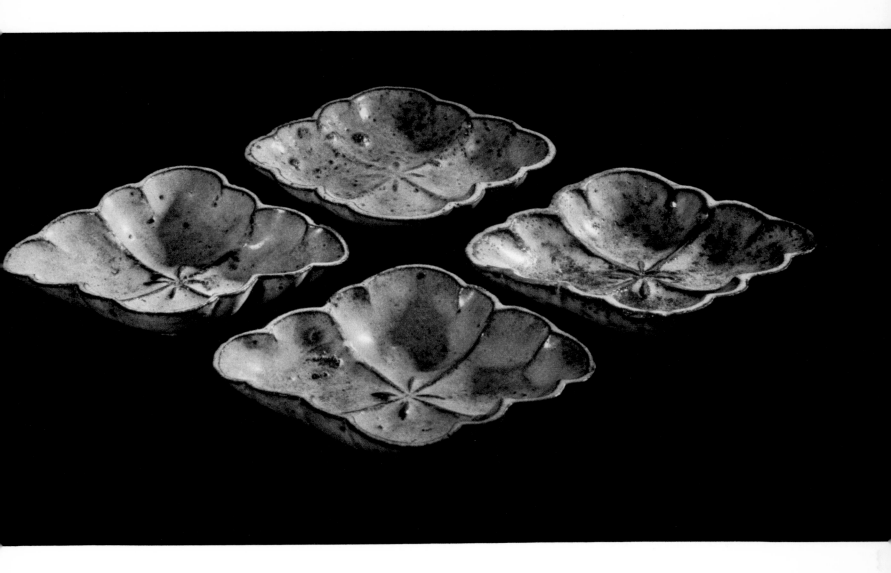

120. TEA BOWL WITH ENAMELED DESIGN

OF MOON AND WAVES BY NINSEI

Height, 3 11/16 in. Diameter, 5 1/8 in. National Museum, Tokyo

This is a representative example of the work of the famous potter Ninsei, who lived and worked in Kyoto during the second half of the seventeenth century. The tea bowl is notable for its elegant form, soft coloring, and simple but sophisticated decoration, all of which seem to be completely in harmony. The ware is a whitish-buff porous clay covered with a thin coat of transparent glaze. The decoration of the waves is applied in a mixture of soft blues and greens and above this the scimitar form of the new moon is drawn in a single sweeping line of iron-brown. The base is inscribed with the two characters of Ninsei's name.

[279]

121. TEA BOWL WITH IRON-BROWN DECORATION

OF PLUM BLOSSOMS BY KENZAN

Height, 3 1/16 in. Diameter, 3 7/8 in. Private Collection

The number of pieces of so-called Kenzan pottery which can reliably be attributed to the great master himself is very small, but this tea bowl is generally considered to be one of them. The body is of a grayish-white porous clay covered with a cloudy translucent glaze, and the design of plum branches and blossoms is painted in a ferruginous black-brown shade under the glaze. The strength and sureness of the brushwork is impressive and extends to the Kenzan signature on the base of the tea bowl.

122. TEAPOT IN THE CHINESE MANNER BY MOKUBEI

Height, 3 ¹³/₁₆ in. Diameter, 4 ¹/₁₆ in. National Museum, Tokyo

Mokubei (1768–1834) was the adopted name of another gifted potter of Kyōyaki wares who followed in the tradition of Ninsei and Kenzan. Although he did not create any original style of great importance, his decorated wares executed in blue and white and in red and green in the Ming manner are highly regarded by Japanese devotees of the tea ceremony. This teapot with design of waves and a fish is one such piece. It is decorated in yellow, green, and brown enamels on a soft whitish clay body very thinly potted. The underpart of the lid and the base are each inscribed with the seal of Mokubei.

A SHORT SURVEY OF THE DEVELOPMENT OF KOREAN CERAMICS

HISTORICAL BACKGROUND

EARLIEST PERIOD

THE origins of the Korean people are obscure, but archaeological remains and linguistic evidence support the theory that the original inhabitants of Korea came primarily from the Tungusic stock of north-central Asia. Soon after 400 B. C. Chinese civilization expanded into neighboring Korea, taking with it a highly developed metal culture, and further Chinese penetration culminated under the Han dynasty in the establishment of a Chinese colony in the territory north of the Han River. This territory was divided into four regions, of which one, surrounding the modern city of Pyongyang, was known as Lolang. Lolang remained a colony of China from the time of its establishment in about 108 B.C. until 313 A.D—well after the end of the Han dynasty—when it fell to the invading armies of the Koguryo kingdom. As might be expected, the Lolang culture was directly derived from that of Han China, and consequently the ceramics of Lolang, though not without their local characteristics, are hardly more than a pale reflection of their contemporary Chinese counterparts.

THE THREE KINGDOMS AND UNIFIED SILLA (57 B. C. – 935 A. D.)

During the period of Chinese dominance in the north, three native states were gradually formed in the Korean peninsula. The strongest of these was Koguryo, in southeastern Manchuria and northern Korea, which derived great advantage both culturally and materially from its proximity to China and Lolang. Koguryo, which adopted a warlike policy toward Lolang, completed the conquest of the country in 313 A.D. and thereafter, becoming increasingly powerful, achieved a prosperity which lasted for the greater part of three centuries. In 427 A.D. the Koguryo capital was moved from Chi-an near the Yalu River to Pyongyang.

The other two states, Paekche and Silla, developed more slowly, receiving part of their cultural stimulus from Koguryo. Paekche was far less military-minded than her warlike neighbors, and her culture, which owed much to the inspiration of the Buddhist faith, reflected influences from China of the Six Dynasties period. Driven by their highly organized and powerful military neighbor, the people of Paekche moved their capital successively southward from Kwangju in Kyonggi-dō to Kyōngju in Chungnam and finally to Puyo in the same province. Despite the ravages of war, the Buddhist culture of Paekche reached a high pinnacle

[285]

of achievement, and in fact it was from this little kingdom (known in Japanese as Kudara) that a host of priests, scholars, artists, and craftsmen went across the sea to Japan to assist in laying the foundations of the new Buddhist culture there.

The third kingdom, Silla, was later than either Koguryo or Paekche in receiving the Buddhist faith but was quicker to develop it, and the ardent response of the Silla nation to Buddhism was accompanied by a rapid rise in the national power and in military strength. Silla, possessing an efficient army, hardened through long years of struggle with Koguryo and Paekche, ultimately succeeded in uniting most of Korea under a single rule in 668 A.D., and the period from this date to the beginning of the Koryō dynasty in 918 is known as the Unified Silla period. There was, however, a small area in the extreme south of the peninsula, referred to as "Kara" in Silla records and "Mimana" in contemporary Japanese histories, which was apparently under Japanese dominance and actual Japanese administration for a large part of the period from early in the fifth century until the year 570 A.D., when it came under the rule of Silla. The enlarged territory of Silla covered only the southern half of the peninsula, the northern frontier with China being the Taetong kang River and the Ch'ŏlyŏng mountains. At this time T'ang China was at the height of her cultural development, and Chinese culture flowed directly into Korea by land, while the sea route from Ningpo was in active use. It is not altogether surprising, then, that the Unified Silla period saw an astonishing cultural development throughout the kingdom.

THE KORYŌ PERIOD (918–1392 A.D.)

Toward the end of the T'ang dynasty the power of Silla began to decline and, in the struggle for power which followed, a Koryō general named Wangkōn proved the strongest among the claimants to the throne. In the year 918 he declared himself king, and in 935 the last Silla ruler abdicated and Wangkōn moved his capital to the city now known as Kaesōng. The Korean nation was thus really unified for the first time and its territory included practically the whole area of the peninsula. The new regime was strongly Buddhist and aristocratic like the old, and its culture was highly centralized in the capital. The neighbors of the newly established state were the Liao Empire in East Mongolia, and a little later the Northern Sung dynasty, which established its rule over China in 960, so that Koryō culture came to be imbued with Liao and Sung elements in addition to those of T'ang China which had been transmitted from Silla. The Koryō dynasty lasted four hundred and seventy-five years under thirty-four kings, and the early part of this period saw the birth of the famous Koryō ceramics. It was only natural that the increasingly intimate contacts with China through the port of Ningpo should have brought to Korea the ceramic technique of the contemporary Yüeh wares of central eastern China, and it was under their influence that the Korean low-fired green-glazed pottery which had been evolved at a number of kilns by the end of the Silla period developed into the early Koryō celadon.

The establishment of the Yi dynasty which followed the Koryō period was not achieved without a considerable political, social, religious, and economic upheaval. The Buddhist faith was abandoned and a type of Confucianism, introduced into Korea at the end of the fourteenth century, became for five hundred years the philosophical mainstay of the Korean state. Nevertheless, although Buddhism was banished from court and capital it survived in more modest form in the country. In the earlier part of the Yi period, the guiding principle of national policy was to maintain harmonious relations with the Ming dynasty, and after the fall of the Ming in 1644 the same policy was instituted with respect to the Ch'ing rulers of China. Except for a period of about forty-three years at the end of the sixteenth and in the early part of the seventeenth century, therefore, when the prosperity of the country was violently disrupted by the invasion (1592–1599) of the Japanese military leader Hideyoshi, and again soon after by the destructive Manchu invasions of 1625 and 1636, Korea under the Yi dynasty enjoyed peace until the last part of the nineteenth century. In general Yi civilization was literary and philosophic, and this outlook is reflected in the pottery of the period, much of which was made not for the use of the Court or for other official purposes but for ordinary everyday use by the people.

THE CERAMIC WARES OF KOREA

GENERAL

To Japanese connoisseurs, Korean pottery of all periods is suggestive of the loneliness of the desolate Korean landscape and full of the melancholy born of the turbulent history of that sad country. Although the wares no doubt owe much to Chinese techniques, they all have an unmistakable Korean quality about them. They avoid showy colors or any display of magnificence and in general are characterized by quietness, modesty, and an artless harmony.

WARES OF THE LOLANG PERIOD (108 B.C.–313 A.D.)

Earthenware vessels of various kinds were made in Korea in prehistoric times, but during the Lolang period low-fired, green-glazed and brown-glazed pottery appears to have been manufactured in considerable quantities for the furnishing of tombs (plate 131). Examples of this ware, which in form and technique closely resembles the Han low-fired glazed pottery, have

[287]

been excavated from ancient tombs near Pyongyang. They comprise tripod vessels, incense burners, models of buildings and wells, and figures of animals and birds. The glaze in nearly all cases has assumed a brownish color as a result of contact with the ferruginous earth in which they were buried.

POTTERY OF THE PERIOD OF THE THREE KINGDOMS (4TH TO 7TH CENTURY A.D.)

There are no surviving wares which can reliably be ascribed to Koguryo, but it seems possible from excavations carried out by Japanese scholars in ancient tomb sites near Pyongyang that the Koguryo people continued to make low-fired glazed earthenwares in the manner of Lolang. In Paekche, on the other hand, the potter's craft evidently flourished, and although the products are mostly degenerate types of Han wares they are more finely potted and elegant than those of Koguryo. The Paekche wares may be divided into four distinct types: (1) reddish-brown and yellowish-brown earthenware figures made of a soft coarse clay fired at a relatively low temperature; (2) pottery vessels of dark-gray or black color made of a fine-grained smooth clay; (3) porcelaneous wares fired at a relatively high temperature—usually dark-gray or greenish-gray in color as a result of smoke in the kiln during firing; and (4) pottery covered with yellowish-brown or yellowish-green glaze, similar to the types found in Lolang and Koguryo tombs near Pyongyang. The number of surviving wares of this last type is small, but there exists one very fine example in the form of a tall-necked green-glazed jar in the possession of the well-known Japanese collector, Mr. Takenosuke Ogura.

The Silla wares of the period before unification of the country in the seventh century are generally referred to as "Old Silla" pottery. Most of the surviving examples were excavated from a group of ancient tombs in the southern outskirts of Kyōngju thought to date from the fifth and sixth centuries. They are dark-gray or blackish pottery fired at a relatively high temperature, and although they are clearly derived from the Han tradition the wares show a surprising mastery of technique and are in a greater variety of forms than Silla wares of later times. During the Unified Silla period, it was the custom to cremate the dead and to deposit the ashes in urns and then bury the urns in the earth. A great proportion of the Silla pottery which has survived is in the form of these urns of black or dark-gray pottery in a number of differing shapes; many of them are decorated with the aid of clay molds, with simple impressed designs of flowers, birds, and grasses.

From the seventh to the ninth century the Silla potters also turned out a low-fired earthenware of a reddish-brown color as well as low-fired green-glazed and brown-glazed pottery of which a relatively large quantity has been excavated. A very fine example of this pottery is a famous green-glazed urn in the Tokyo National Museum.

In the small Japanese colony in the extreme south of the Korean peninsula, referred to as Kara in Silla records and as Mimana in the *Nihon Shoki* (Chronicles of Japan), a grayish-black earthenware was made during the fifth and sixth centuries. Although this ware is in most respects indistinguishable from Silla pottery of the period, some of it is of rather finer execution and finish (plate 132).

THE KORYŌ WARES

The Koryō period (918–1392) was the golden age of Korean ceramics and witnessed the production of some of the most beautiful glazed pottery the world has ever seen. The Koryō celadons are particularly famous, and deservedly so, for at their best they are in no way inferior to the finest of Chinese Sung wares in form and glaze, while the originality and imagination displayed in the decorative technique is nothing short of breath-taking (plates 123, 124, 125, and 133).

Although there are a very few pieces of Koryō ware which are known to have been in Japan for several centuries, the great majority of the surviving wares of Koryō have emerged only comparatively recently from tombs of the Koryō period, as the wares were buried with their owners and recovered only in the early part of this century, mostly in a frantic burst of surreptitious digging in the numerous graves of the Kaesong area. A large proportion of the many thousands of pieces thus recovered is therefore, alas, undocumented, but as a result of much patient research on the part of Japanese scholars during the last thirty or forty years it is now possible to classify the wares according to types and period of manufacture, and even in many cases to identify with reasonable confidence the district in which they were made. In the light of this research the history of ceramic production during the Koryō period falls naturally into four main parts:

1. The first period, from the early part of the tenth century until about the beginning of the eleventh century, when ceramic production was apparently limited to the manufacture of wares closely resembling the Silla pottery, including high-fired semiporcelaneous urns and low-fired green-glazed and yellowish-brown-glazed articles. Examples which can be definitely dated to this period are few in number, but Mr. Ken Nomori in his "Study of Koryō Wares" refers to a green-glazed urn dated the 22nd year of Hyun-jong (1031).

2. A period of about a hundred and sixty years between the eighth king, Hyun-jong (1010–1032), and the eighteenth king, Eui-jong (1147–1171), when pottery was made in imitation of contemporary Chinese wares. The light gray-green and greenish-brown celadons made early in this period clearly show the influence of the Yüeh Chou wares of the T'ang period. Later, as Korean ceramic technique continued to improve, a beautiful jade-green glaze was evolved and the products came close to attaining the perfection of the high-quality Yüeh celadon wares of the Five Dynasties and early Sung periods. It is difficult to date this development

precisely, but the generally accepted opinion is that the Koryō potters were turning out plain undecorated celadon in the Chinese manner during the period between the eleventh king, Mun-jong (1047–1083), and the fifteenth king, Suk-jong (1096–1106). By the time of the sixteenth king, Ye-jong (1106–1123), the kilns were making not only the plain celadons but also celadon wares with engraved decoration under the glaze. At this time also, white porcelain was produced, as well as celadons painted in a black ferruginous clay under the glaze known to the Japanese as *egorai*. The forms, technique, and decoration of these wares clearly indicate that they were inspired by such well-known Chinese wares of the Northern Sung dynasty as Ting yao, Ju yao, Tz'ū Chou yao, and Ching-tê-chên yao.

3. The period which saw the introduction and perfection of peculiarly Korean wares covers about a hundred and sixty years between the eighteenth king, Eui-jong (1147–1171), and the twenty-fifth king, Chung-yul-wang (1275–1309). In the early part of this period the Koryō potters broke away from the dominating influence of Chinese ceramics and created new forms and styles which are wholly Korean in inspiration. It was at about this time that inlaid decoration was introduced or at least first came to be used widely, and although no precise date can yet be advanced for the invention of this technique, it must have been in vogue soon after the middle of the twelfth century, as two fine inlaid celadons were excavated from a tomb containing a stone casket on which there was a lengthy epitaph and a date corresponding to the year 1159. Both these pieces were of such advanced workmanship that they are unlikely to have been the earliest productions of their kind. This period also saw the development of such typically Korean forms as the long-necked vases and gourd-shaped vases and pitchers, and the two famous traditional Korean patterns, one of cranes and flying clouds and the other of willows and water-fowl, which were destined to be used over and over again in the decoration of the inlaid celadons. There does not seem to have been any marked deterioration in the quality of inlaid celadon ware up to the end of the twelfth century, for specimens recovered from the tomb of King Myung-jong, who died in 1197, were of high quality, and a comparative study of shards from kiln sites has left little doubt that this was the peak period of ceramic production, when the Koryō potteries were at the height of their prosperity. After about the middle of the thirteenth century, however, the striving for decorative effect led rapidly to the adoption of more pretentious designs and the extravagant use of ornament. No doubt this was partly caused by the influence of the Mongols, who swept over the country in successive waves of invasion from the year 1231, but it led to a gradual decline which was to become more rapid after the turn of the fourteenth century.

4. The last eighty years of the Koryō period, ending with the overthrow of the dynasty in 1392, were a time of degeneration and decline with no further progress. Celadons of various types, including the wares decorated with iron-brown or black slip designs under the glaze, and almost all other kinds of Koryō ceramics continued to be made, but they tended to be

crude in workmanship, glaze, and firing. The celadon glaze took on a grayish-green or grayish-brown color sadly inferior to the beautiful jade-green and turquoise colors of the past. However, it was this lamentable degradation which led later on in the time of the Yi dynasty to wares of great charm and originality known to the Koreans as Punch'ŏng wares and to the Japanese as Mishima-de.

Mr. Ken Nomori divides all the known ceramic products of the Koryŏ period into fifteen types, classified as follows:

1. The unglazed pottery of Silla type which was turned out in large quantities for the daily use of the people.

2. Low-fired green-glazed and yellowish-brown-glazed pottery which was already in production at the beginning of the Koryŏ period and continued to be made at least until the reign of the tenth king, Cheong-yong (1035–1047).

3. The plain and incised celadon wares which, as indicated previously, were made in an ever-increasing variety of styles from about the middle of the eleventh century until the end of the Koryŏ period (plates 123 and 133).

4. The inlaid celadons, manufacture of which probably began shortly before the middle of the twelfth century (plates 124, 125, and 136).

5. Celadons with decoration painted in iron-brown or black slip under the glaze. These are thought to have been first made in imitation of the wares of Tz'ŭ Chou yao during the reign of the fifteenth king, Suk-jong (1096–1106).

6. Celadons modeled and incised under the glaze with plain lines to create or suggest the shape of, for example, a melon or a bamboo shoot (plate 123). Many of these take the form of pillows, ewers, or vases. They appear to have been made from the time of the eleventh king, Mun-jong (1047–1083), onward until the end of the thirteenth century.

7. White wares, both plain and with engraved decoration (plates 134 and 135), manufacture of which started in the reign of the sixteenth king, Yo-jong (1106–1123), and continued even after the end of the Koryŏ dynasty.

8. Iron-black celadon wares, which were first made in the time of the twentieth king, Shin-jong (1198–1205). These are often mistaken for black-glazed pottery, but in fact they were made by applying a ferruginous black slip on the body and covering it all over with a thin coating of celadon glaze. Some examples have simple designs of white flowers or cranes in reserve, made by scraping off the iron slip (plate 138).

9. Iron-brown wares covered with a glaze of high ferruginous content which has assumed a reddish-brown color during firing. Some of these have simple decorations in reserve.

10. Iron-black glazed wares covered with a dark-brown or black glaze, which are called by the Japanese *Kōrai-temmoku* (plate 137). Depending on the firing conditions, some of the wares have a dull glaze finish while others are quite glossy. These wares are thought to date from

as early as the twentieth king, Shin-jong (1198–1205), but most of the surviving specimens in this category are products of the latter part of the Koryŏ period.

11. Celadon wares with underglaze-red decoration. Unlike the Chinese wares of Chün yao which often have large splashes of copper, the Koryŏ wares, termed *shinsha* by the Japanese, usually have a pattern of red dots under a celadon glaze, and it is rare to find designs drawn in the copper-red color. This type of ware, according to Mr. Nomori, was originated in the time of the twentieth king, Shin-jong (1198–1205), and ceased to be made after about the reign of the twenty-fifth king, Chung-yul-wang (1275–1309). Nearly all the surviving wares of this type are thought to date from the latter period.

12. Celadon wares inlaid with white and black clays and with gilded decoration. Surviving wares of this type, which were first made during the reign of the twenty-third king, Ko-jong (1204–1260), are very rare indeed. It is thought that they ceased to be made by the end of the thirteenth century.

13. Lacquered pottery. Only one piece of this type is known to have survived. It is in the collection of the Duksoo Palace Museum of Fine Arts in Seoul.

14. Marbled wares made of a mixture of red or gray clay with white clay in the Chinese manner, covered with a thin celadon glaze. Among the wares of this type which have survived are a small number of covered boxes, wine cups, and small pots.

15. Sundry glazed wares made toward the end of the Koryŏ period, among which may be found wares covered with a variety of different-colored glazes, including amber, straw color, and a yellowish-green.

Almost all the major kiln sites of the Koryŏ period have been discovered in the course of the past fifty years. The principal centers of ceramic production numbered no less than eighteen throughout the country, the two most important being at Kangjin, in the southwestern corner of the peninsula, where about ninety kiln sites have been discovered, and at Puan, some eighty miles to the north, where about seventy kiln sites were found.

WARES OF THE YI DYNASTY (1392–1910)

Speaking objectively, the Korean ceramics of the Yi dynasty are degenerate types of the Koryŏ wares, and they cannot compete with the latter in elegance of form, workmanship, or decorative technique. Nevertheless they achieve a quiet beauty of their own, and their simplicity of form together with a certain artlessness evident in their manufacture recommends them to devotees of the tea ceremony. Some of the Yi wares display great originality and humor in the decoration, and nearly all have a special charm of a kind which is not to be found in more sophisticated pottery and porcelain.

In Chinese ceramics, changes in the time and in the affairs of the court and the people are in general sharply reflected in the styles and modes of each period, but this is not true in the case of Korean wares of the Yi period, where the distinction of styles is blurred and the difference between the products of one age and another is often difficult to perceive. One reason for this is no doubt the conservatism and phlegmatic nature of the Korean people; and of course the fact that very few of the Yi period wares bear any period inscription makes the problem of dating doubly hard. A great deal of work has been done in this field by Japanese scholars, however.

Mr. Hakkyo Asakawa, who is perhaps the outstanding authority on the subject, has classified ceramics of the Yi dynasty chronologically as follows:

The Early Epoch (period of contact with Ming culture)

First period (first year of the reign of King Tae-jo [1392] to the seventh year of the reign of King Se-jo [1463]). The official porcelain and pottery factories were established, and produced large quantities of Punch'ong ware (termed by the Japanese *mishima*) in a variety of different techniques and decorations, as well as white porcelain and iron-brown (*temmoku*) glazed wares.

Second period (eighth year of King Se-jo [1464] to the thirty-first year of the reign of King Seonjo [1598]). During most of this period the official kilns prospered exceedingly and produced, in addition to the earlier type of wares, blue-and-white decorated porcelain of high quality. A number of local private kilns were also active at this time, turning out tea bowls, porcelain with iron-oxide painting and copper-red painting under the glaze, and grayish pottery inlaid with white slip or decorated with white clay.

Third period (thirty-second year of the reign of King Seon-jo [1599] to the forty-third year of the reign of King Suk-jong [1717]). The beginning of this period saw a marked change in Korean ceramic production resulting from the devastation of the country by the soldiers of the Japanese despot Toyotomi Hideyoshi, who invaded Korea between 1592 and 1598. Close on the heels of the war came a great famine, and in the fourteenth year of the reign of King In-jo (1636) Korea was again invaded, this time by the armies of the Manchus. As a result of this series of unhappy events the people were reduced to great misery, which was reflected in the degeneration of the products of the time, including pottery. Most of the official factories were devastated; some types of pottery, including that of the "brushed-slip" group, went out of existence, and porcelain wares also declined. Because of the scarcity of imported cobalt for the underglaze blue decoration, wares with underglaze iron-browns and copper-reds became

[293]

the main products of the remaining official kilns, and the local private factories all but gave up the production of high-fired wares.

The Later Epoch (period of contact with Ch'ing culture)

First period (forty-fourth year of the reign of King Suk-jong [1718] to the twenty-seventh year of the reign of King Yeong-jo [1751]). In 1718 a branch of the official factory was established at Keumsa-ri near Kwangju, Kyonggi-dō. This branch factory evidently prospered, for within a few years it became the principal ceramic-manufacturing center of Korea. The majority of Yi period blue-and-white wares now in existence probably date from this or the following period. They are characterized by very simple drawing of the decoration, in a grayish-blue pigment made from unrefined cobalt.

Second period (twenty-eighth year of King Yeong-jo [1752] to the twentieth year of the reign of King Ko-jong [1883]). This period marks a fresh upsurge of cultural development in Korea, when the official branch kiln, reaching the peak of its achievement, produced wares of great technical excellence but with excessively elaborate decoration. Generally speaking, the products of the official factory at this time may be identified by their dull glazes with a bluish or grayish tinge and the over-intricate decoration and profuse use of underglaze blue. The forms and designs tend to be perplexingly artful.

Third period. This period begins in 1884, the twenty-first year of the reign of King Ko-jong, when the Yi Government, harassed by financial difficulties, converted the official branch factory into a private undertaking. Thereafter, the use of industrial cobalt began, the method of applying decoration by the copper-plate lithographic process was introduced, and the forms and designs of Korean ceramics became muddled and lifeless, with the result that in a short space of time the tradition of ceramic manufacture in Korea was lost.

The variety of wares made during the Yi dynasty was certainly great, and the quantity turned out must have been enormous, but as they were for the most part used in the daily life of the people—unlike the Koryō celadons, which it seems were made as ornaments for burial with their owners—only a small proportion has survived the hazards and vicissitudes of ordinary existence in Korea.

Few, if any, of the Yi period pottery pieces were preserved by contemporary Korean collectors, and in fact it is only since the beginning of this century that a relatively small number of pieces of the earlier Yi wares which by some miracle had escaped destruction came into the hands of Korean and Japanese connoisseurs, who have since cherished and preserved them. In view of the hundreds of pottery centers operating in Korea during the Yi period and the paucity of surviving examples, the detailed classification of Yi wares by types presents extraordinary difficulties, but they may be broadly separated into eleven groups as follows:

1. The so-called *Mishima* or Punch'ŏng ware, most of which is a dark-gray-bodied ware covered all over with a white inlaid or white-painted slip design of dots or else covered with a coating of white slip and decorated under the transparent glaze with iron oxide (plate 139). The finest of all these in workmanship and finish are the wares made for presentation to the government as taxes in kind, called by the Japanese *Reihinmishima*.

2. The carved or engraved Punch'ŏng wares, similar in body and technique of potting and glazing to the above but with bold designs engraved deeply into the body and filled with white clay (plate 126). These seem to have been made in the southern part of Cholla province.

3. Dark-gray-bodied wares similar to the above but with decoration applied in white slip with swift, sure brush strokes.

4. Punch'ŏng-type wares covered with a coat of white slip and decorated with figures of flowers, birds, and fish in reserve by the sgraffito technique (plate 140). This kind of pottery has been found both in Cholla-namdō and in ancient tombs on Cheju Island.

5. Wares very similar to the above but with the designs painted on the white slip in underglaze iron oxide. These wares appear to have been made in Cholla-namdō also, but there they were fired at a lower temperature and the designs were less attractive than similar decorated pottery produced at a kiln near Mount Kyeryong, some distance away (plate 141).

6. Black-glazed wares, referred to by the Japanese as Yi period *temmoku*, which seem to have been made at a great number of kilns throughout Korea in the first part and again in the latter part of the Yi dynasty. The best of these have a thick semi-mat glaze and are highly prized by connoisseurs of the tea ceremony.

7. White-glazed wares, which, like the black wares, were made all over Korea throughout the Yi period. They were produced in large quantities and surviving examples are relatively plentiful. The major centers of production were Kongju in Kyonggi-dō, about twenty miles east of Seoul, and Koyong in southern Kyongsang province.

8. Blue-and-white porcelains. The manufacture of blue-and-white wares in quantity was probably started about the middle of the fifteenth century, when the main center of production was Kwangju, southeast of Seoul (plate 146). The best period of Korean blue-and-white, however, was probably the first half of the eighteenth century, shortly after the establishment of the official branch factory at Keumsa-ri.

9. Coarse porcelaneous pottery with simple rough designs painted in iron oxide under a bluish transparent glaze (plate 130). These wares were made mainly in private kilns situated in North Korea from about the middle of the Yi period.

10. White porcelaneous wares with decoration in underglaze copper-red (plate 129). Wares

with this type of decoration, which was presumably inspired by Ming underglaze-red porcelain, appear to have been made even before the blue-and-white wares, as examples which can be reliably dated to the first part of the Yi dynasty have been excavated from kiln sites in Kwangju. However, the majority of the surviving wares with this type of decoration probably date from the eighteenth century.

11. Miscellaneous pottery, including those wares of the Yi dynasty which do not fall into any of the preceding categories, and also, besides degraded types of Koryō celadon, several varieties of tea bowls known in Japan as *Kōraijawan* or *Chōsenjawan*, highly prized by the devotees of the tea ceremony.

123. KORYŌ CELADON WINE POT

IN THE FORM OF A BAMBOO SHOOT

Height, 9 ¹/₂ in. Diameter, 3 9/₁₆ in. Private Collection

This lovely creation, which is among the finest of all existing Koryō celadons, is thought to be a product of the Imperial kilns in the period between the reigns of the seventeenth Koryō ruler, In-jong (1125–1147), and the nineteenth ruler, Myung-jong (1171–1198)—a period which has been called the golden age of Koryō wares. The fine Koryō celadons which the Chinese traveler Hsü Ching extolled in his record of a journey to Korea in 1124, and which are praised by implication in a Chinese work* of the Sung dynasty, were no doubt of this kind and quality.

The body is a light-gray porcelaneous ware with a trace of iron content, and the whole, including the foot, is entirely covered with an even coat of cool green celadon glaze of perfect texture. The ewer is molded in the form of a growing bamboo shoot, while the spout and the handle have been modeled to represent bamboo cane.

While there are a number of similar ewers of bamboo-shoot design in Japan and also in collections in Europe and America, for perfection of form and glaze none can match this one, which is truly an artistic triumph. It was probably made at one of the two factories of the Koryō dynasty which are particularly noted for the excellence of their celadon products: that is, the kiln at Sadang-ri, in the Kangjin district, and the Yu-cheon-ri kiln, in the Puan district.

*The *Hsiu Chung Chin,* a literary work of the Sung period which seems to have disappeared, but which is mentioned in a Korean historical work of the Yi dynasty entitled *Haedong Yoksa.* The passage in question reads: "The books of the Academy, the wines of the palace, the inkstones of Huichou Fu, the peonies of Lo-yang, the tea of Chien-chou, and the *pi se* [secret color, i. e. celadon] of Koryō are all the first under Heaven."

124. KORYŌ CELADON LARGE GLOBULAR JAR

WITH INLAID DECORATION OF PEONIES AND ARABESQUES

Height, 8 11/16 in.   Diameter, 10 3/8 in.   Private Collection

This jar is notable for the perfection of its amply modeled form and for the exquisite inlaid decoration, which takes the form of peonies in double circles surrounded by a band of trefoils and graceful arabesques executed in inlaid black and white clays. The stylized peony scrolls filling the space between the two principal decorative motifs are unusually beautiful and harmoniously balanced. The smooth, even-textured celadon glaze is of a grayish hue, which may perhaps be counted a defect, but the jar is nevertheless an object of great beauty, and its superb workmanship is representative of the finest period of Koryō celadon manufacture in the second half of the twelfth century.

Like the wine pot of in bamboo-shoot design in plate 123, this piece was probably made at either Sadang-ri or Yu-cheon-ri.

125. KORYŌ CELADON WINE POT DECORATED IN
THE RESERVE METHOD AND BLACK INLAY

Height, 7 9/16 in. Private Collection

This wine pot has a charming design of grapevines and baby boys outlined in black inlay on a grayish-green ground effected by a decorative technique frequently used in China but seldom seen in Koryō celadons. The piece was first covered all over with a coat of white slip which was scraped off in the *sgraffito* manner to reserve the area where the design was to be applied; the outlines of the grapevine and the infants were then engraved in the body and filled with black clay, and the whole pot was covered with a soft celadon glaze and then fired.

This remarkable piece first came to note when Hobson published it in an issue of the *Burlington Magazine* for April, 1950 (Issue No. 325). It seems that it was on display in an exhibition of old Korean ceramics held at Taegu in 1929 when the celebrated English scholar happened to be visiting Korea.

Although it is not possible to attach a precise date of manufacture to this wine pot, it is safe to assume that it must have been made at about the end of the twelfth century in the time of the nineteenth ruler, Myung-jong (1171–1198), or the twentieth ruler, Shin-jong (1198–1205). From the fact that shards with a very similar type of decoration have been found at No. 17 kiln at Yu-cheon-ri, it seems possible that it was made in that neighborhood, or else conceivably at Sadang-ri in the Kangjin district.

126. WINE BOTTLE WITH DESIGN OF PEONIES INCISED

AND PAINTED IN WHITE SLIP

Height, 13 9/16 in. Private Collection

The pleasing, bold decoration of this bottle was made by incising the pattern very slightly but broadly into the grayish pottery body and filling with white slip. The glaze is transparent white with a tinge of green and is crackled all over. It is difficult to date this type of ware, which is considered by some authorities to have been made at the end of the Koryō period, but on the evidence provided by an incised and painted funerary urn of this type excavated from a tomb in the precincts of a temple named Song-Kwa-sa at Sooncheon in South Cholla province it may be more correct to consider the ware as belonging to the early part of the Yi period. The urn in question contained the ashes of Kobong-whasang, a Buddhist monk who died in the tenth year of King Se-jong of the Yi dynasty (1428). A rather large number of fine incised and painted wares of this kind, including bowls and covered boxes, have been recovered from Cheju Island, and this bottle is perhaps from there, but it is thought that the place of manufacture was in the district of Hampyung, Kwangju.

127. WATERPOT WITH *KOHIKI*-TYPE GLAZE

Height, 6 1/16 in. Diameter, 7 5/16 in. Private Collection

Pottery wares of this type, which were probably made at various kilns in South Cholla province during the early part of the Yi dynasty, have been preserved for centuries in Japan, where they are highly appreciated for use in the tea ceremony. The water-pot illustrated here is of a ferruginous grayish-brown clay coated with the distinctive thick "warm-white" slip of South Korean kilns of the Yi dynasty, over which a white transparent glaze is applied. The resultant powdery texture of the glaze has given rise in Japan to the term *kohiki* (powder).

128. "PILGRIM FLASK" WINE BOTTLE

PAINTED IN UNDERGLAZE BLUE (YI DYNASTY)

Height, 7 15/16 in. Private Collection

This wine bottle enjoys high favor among Japanese connoisseurs of pottery for the quality of unaffected simplicity apparent in its form, glaze, and decoration. On the side shown in the illustration a design of pinks is painted in cobalt under the glaze, and the reverse side is similarly decorated with a bold composition of pomegranates. It is a grayish-white porcelaneous ware covered with a thick semiopaque white glaze with mat surface. This piece was perhaps made during the eighteenth century at the Keumsa-ri kiln in Kwangju.

129. BOTTLE VASE WITH DECORATION IN UNDERGLAZE RED

Height, 10 11/16 in. Private Collection

The form of this vase, with the curving surface from neck to base faceted octagonally, is one found frequently in Yi period Korean pottery. This rare example, with
a design of a hawk on a pine tree and a human figure painted in bright copper-red
under the thick bluish-white glaze, is particularly celebrated. The technique of
painting in copper-red under the glaze was started in Koryō times and was widely
employed during the Yi dynasty, but usually only in combination with underglaze
blue, which was evidently a much easier color to control in the kiln. The principal
center of production of the underglaze copper-red wares was at Keumsa-ri in
Kwangju, but they were also made at other places, including Kyodong in
Hamkyung-namdo. This vase is thought to have been made at Keumsa-ri toward
the end of the seventeenth century.

130. JAR WITH UNDERGLAZE IRON-BROWN DECORATION

Height, 9 in. Private Collection

This jar is one of the most beautiful of known examples of the relatively plentiful underglaze iron-brown decorated wares of the Yi dynasty. The body is a fine-quality white porcelain covered with a white glaze faintly tinged with blue. The freely drawn design reminiscent of a spray of orchids is applied in dark-brown iron oxide under the glaze, and judging by its quality it is the work of an artist rather than a mere craftsman.

Wares decorated in this manner with iron oxide under the glaze were evidently made throughout the Yi period at a large number of factories located all over Korea, but according to Dr. N. Asakawa this piece is thought to be a product of the Mirok-ri kiln, situated at Sangmo-myun, Koesan-gun, in North Chung-cheong province. It came to light in about 1928, presumably as a result of surreptitious digging, and unfortunately the place where it was excavated is not known; but Dr. Asakawa places it among the products of the middle Yi period.

131. LOLANG GREEN-GLAZED INCENSE BURNER

Height, 7 15/16 in. Private Collection

The illustration shows an example of the low-fired green-glazed ware produced in the neighborhood of the modern city of Pyongyang during the period of the Chinese colony of Lolang (108 B. C. – 303 A. D.). As may be seen, in form, style, and glazing it closely resembles the well-known green-glazed pottery "hill jars" of Han China. However, the body is reddish-brown and the glaze color of a somewhat softer and brighter tone than that of the Han wares. Excavation of Lolang period tomb sites has yielded a number of pieces of pottery of this type, including cups, incense burners, models of buildings and wells, besides figures of birds, all modeled in the style of their contemporary Chinese originals, but exhibiting a markedly lower standard of technical competence.

132.   UNGLAZED POTTERY FROM THE "MIMANA" REGION

Figure on horseback: height, 3 3/16 in.; vessel with two cartwheels:

height, 6 5/8 in.   Private Collection

During the period of the Three Kingdoms (fourth to sixth centuries) a small group of minor states existed on the west bank of the Naktong River in the extreme south of Korea, which were under Japanese administration. The territory is referred to in ancient Japanese records as Mimana. The two pieces illustrated here are representative of some of the unglazed pottery models which have been excavated at various tomb sites in this territory. In general, the so-called Mimana pottery is a high-fired, thinly potted, dark-gray ware closely resembling the Japanese Sueki pottery and the Korean Silla wares, from which it is indeed almost indistinguishable.

The figure on horseback, modeled with feeling and humor, was excavated from a site in Kyongsang-bukdo. Figures similar to this have also been recovered from sites around Kyongju.

The second object is a vessel of unusual form with two cylindrical cups or containers on a rounded stem, and an axis on which is mounted a pair of wheels. It is difficult to determine what it was intended to represent, although it is presumably derived from some kind of wheeled cart. Among the murals discovered in tombs of the Koguryo dynasty, some depict bullock-drawn carts and similar vehicles which seem to have been used at that time for the carriage of the nobility as well as for general transport purposes, and this object is perhaps intended as a sort of drinking vessel using the cart motif.

It is of hard, dark-gray, high-fired pottery, and the workmanship shows a degree of technical excellence surprising in such an early piece. It is said to have been excavated near Changryung in South Kyongsang province.

133. KORYŌ CELADON WATER POURER

WITH ENGRAVED DESIGN OF LOTUS FLOWERS

Height, 10 5/8 in. Nezu Art Gallery, Tokyo

This celebrated water pourer is decorated with an engraved design under the glaze in a manner called by the Japanese *inkoku*. It is of a type associated with the two districts of Kangjin in South Cholla province and Puan in North Cholla province, which, as already noted (plates 123 and 124), are held to have produced the best of the famous celadons of the Koryō period.

The form of the vessel, which is also seen in T'ang pottery as well as in bronze of the Koryō period, is presumably of ritualistic significance, and although its exact purpose is not known it is thought to have been made during the first half of the twelfth century, when Buddhism was flourishing in Korea, for use in Buddhist ceremonial, perhaps as a water sprinkler. The body is a grayish porcelaneous ware, covered with a beautiful jade-green celadon glaze with a crackled surface through which may be seen the delicate design of lotus-flower scrolls, evidently incised by a master hand. On the base, three characters are inscribed under the glaze, recording the name of the engraver. Only two other Koryō pieces are known which bear the maker's name in this manner.

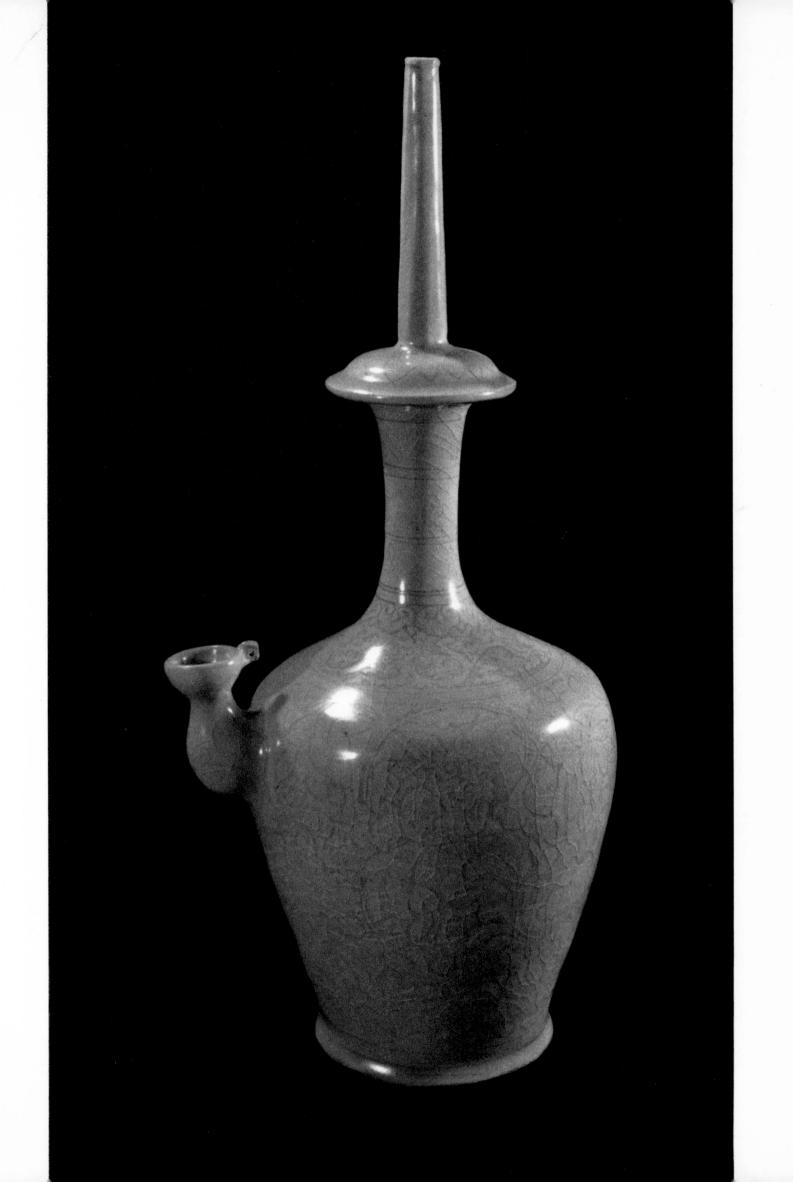

134. KORYŌ WHITE PORCELAIN WINE POT

WITH ENGRAVED DESIGN OF LOTUS SCROLLS

Height, 9 1/4 in. Private Collection

The wine pot illustrated here is perhaps the finest known example of Koryō white ware. The form is remarkable and the decoration beautifully executed; indeed, at first glance the piece might easily be taken for a Chinese product of the Northern Sung period, but closer inspection of the body and the crackled glaze reveals the special characteristics of Koryō white ware. While no doubt inspired by early Sung wares, the form is different from any Chinese piece we have seen, although the modeling of the graceful spout and the handle is reminiscent of that of some early Sung Yüeh wares. The beautiful moldings which mark the extent of the shoulder and the base above the foot are extraordinarily cleanly potted, and the whole is completed with a cover surmounted by an ornamental finial in the shape of a Buddhist jewel.

The body is a chalky-white, rather coarse porcelain, thinly covered with a coat of transparent white glaze minutely crazed on the surface. Beneath the glaze an intricate design of peony scrolls carved in relief covers the whole body of the pot.

Remains of kilns which produced white wares in Koryō times have been discovered at a number of places in Korea, among which the most important seem to have been Yu-cheon-ri, in the Puan district of North Cholla province, and No-am-ri, in the Yeong-heung area of South Hamkyung province, as well as the Koryung area in North Kyongsang and Chinju in South Kyongsang.

Judging from its style, this wine pot is, however, a product of the Puan district and was probably made during the golden age of Koryō ceramic production—that is to say, in the reigns of the seventeenth, eighteenth, and nineteenth rulers, which lasted from 1123 to 1197.

135.   KORYŌ WHITE PORCELAIN WINE VESSEL

WITH INCISED AND INLAID DESIGN

Height, 4 1/8 in.   Diameter, 7 11/16 in.   Private Collection

This wine vessel, which is of unusual shape, has a design of twin birds in flight inlaid in thin lines of black clay in a flattened roundel at the top and is delicately engraved with five floral sprays around the shoulders.   Like the wine pot in plate 134, the vessel has a chalky-white porcelaneous body thinly covered with a greenish-tinted, transparent, white glaze, which is finely crackled all over its surface.   The mouth is precisely potted, as is the wide low foot.

This piece, which is hitherto unpublished, is thought to be a product of the Puan district and was perhaps made at the Yu-cheon-ri kiln.   It is very difficult to say when it was made, but the end of the twelfth century may be a reasonable guess.

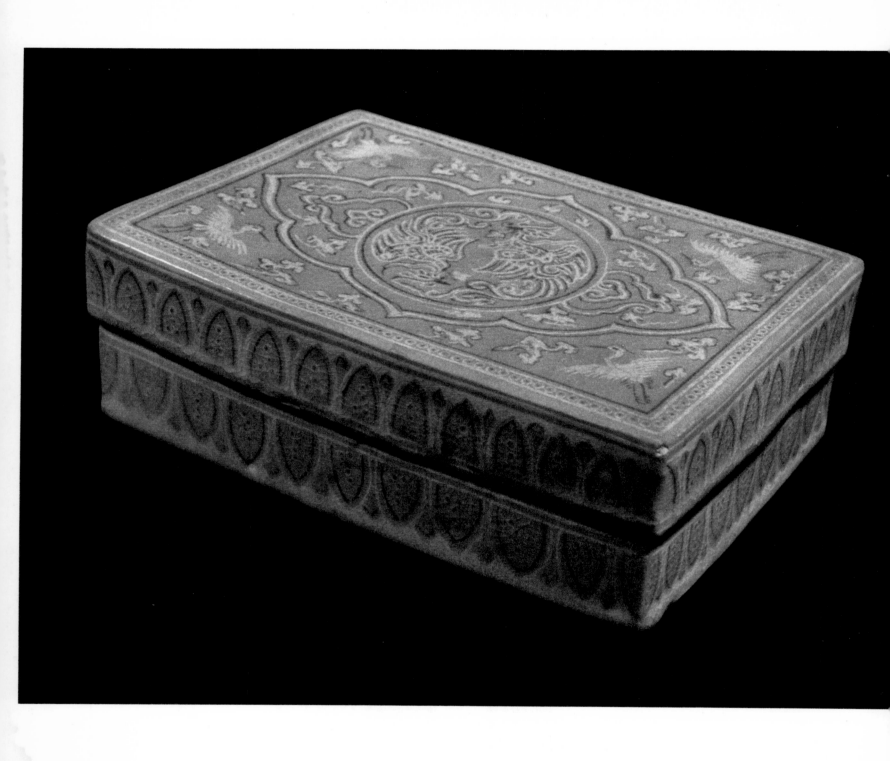

136.   KORYŌ CELADON RECTANGULAR BOX WITH COVER

Length, 8 5/8 in.   Private Collection

This is a remarkably fine example of Koryō inlaid celadon with intricate but beautifully balanced decoration and a lovely bluish-green celadon glaze. In this case the firing must have been perfect, for the glaze is of an even color all over, and unblemished. The inside of the box is plain celadon green. The grayish-white porcelaneous body is relatively thick and heavy, presumably to ensure that the box and its cover would not become warped during firing; and the flat unglazed base is burned reddish-black. Judging from the high quality and careful workmanship, it seems reasonable to regard this box as a product of the period of the nineteenth king, Myung-jong (1171–1198), or the twentieth king, Shin-jong (1198–1205); it was probably made either at Kangjin or at Puan.

Only four boxes of Koryō celadon of this size and shape are known, and three of these, including the one illustrated here, are in Japan. The fourth, which was formerly in the National Museum of Korea, has the design of a tortoise in inlay and openwork decoration. They were all probably made as cosmetic boxes to hold a set of oil jars and containers for powder and rouge.

137. KORYŌ BLACK-GLAZED *(TEMMOKU)* GOURD-SHAPED BOTTLE

Height, 16 9/16 in. Yamato Bunka-kan Museum, Nara

This Koryō *temmoku* bottle, which is judged to be the finest known example of its kind, is notable for the classic beauty of its gourd-shaped form and for the restraint and charm of the dull blackish-brown glaze. The body is a coarse gray earthenware, and the surface is evenly covered with a dark-brown, almost black glaze. The low foot, which is unglazed, is slightly concave.

Black-glazed wares were made at a great many places in the southern part of Korea from Koryō times and throughout the Yi dynasty, but this bottle has the appearance of a Koryō piece, and its style and technique of manufacture are not dissimilar to shards which have been found at kiln sites in the Kangjin district of South Cholla province, famous as the source of some of the fine Koryō celadons. It was perhaps made toward the latter part of the Koryō dynasty, but the perfection of its form postulates a period before the end of the thirteenth century, which marks the beginning of a decline in the quality of Koryō ceramics.

138. BLACK KORYŌ *MAEBYŌNG* (*MEI P'ING*) VASE

WITH DESIGN OF GINSENG LEAVES

Height, 11 7/16 in. Private Collection

This very beautiful vase is an example of an unusual and peculiarly Korean technique. It may appear at first glance to be covered with a black glaze, but in fact the effect was achieved by a different method. Underglaze iron was brushed on the ferruginous earthenware body, next came a mixture of iron and ash to create the deep color, and finally the whole was glazed with transparent celadon. To decorate the vase, the potter incised a spray of ginseng leaves very slightly into the body on both sides and then brushed white slip into these areas.

In places where the glaze has run thinly, the color is brownish in tone. The base is very slightly pared away to leave a low foot-rim.

It is not known just where wares of this type were made, but they do not seem to have been turned out at Kangjin or Puan. Perhaps there was a kiln or group of kilns in South Korea which specialized in the production of such pottery, but up to the present none has been identified. For the same reason they cannot be reliably dated, though the general consensus is that they were made during the thirteenth century.

139. WATER JAR OF PUNCH'ŌNG WARE (YI DYNASTY)

Height, 7 3/16 in. Diameter, 7 5/8 in. Nezu Art Gallery, Tokyo

This water jar is of a type greatly favored for use in the tea ceremony. It has a body of coarse ferruginous clay on which is stamped a design of fleck marks resembling a coarsely woven mesh. The stamped impressions are filled with white slip and the whole is covered with a thick transparent celadon glaze of grayish hue. The swelling globular form and the well-balanced large foot give the jar an air of weight and dignity. It was probably made in Kyongsang province during the early part of the Yi dynasty, that is to say between 1420 and 1470, the period when Punch'ōng (known to the Japanese as *Mishima*) pottery was at its best. It is perhaps questionable, however, whether the jar was originally made in the shape in which we now see it, because the unbalance of the design at the mouth looks slightly odd. It is conjectured that the piece may first have been made in the form of a bottle, and that having had the top damaged it was cut at the shoulder, glazed, and refired. The form is certainly unique in this type of ware.

140. MODEL OF A SHRINE IN PUNCH'ŌNG WARE
WITH ENGRAVED DECORATION

Height, 6 1/16 in. Length, 7 in. Nezu Art Gallery, Tokyo

This pottery shrine is the only known example of its kind. It is a coarse gray ware of ferruginous clay decorated all over with designs inlaid in white clay, and covered with a relatively thick, roughly crackled, transparent glaze with a faint greenish tinge. It is difficult to determine if it was intended as a model of a real building, although the form of the ridgepole makes it appear as if it were. The base is now flat but shows traces of chipping all over the under surface, indicating that the original form was different, and it may perhaps have had a foot or even a second story. On the left of the "door" is an inscription in white-clay inlay, reading "Keumrome-Sa" (temple) followed by one more character which is indecipherable.

It is difficult to determine whether this piece was made in Koryō times or early in the Yi period, but it probably comes from a kiln in South Cholla province.

[333]

141. "KYERYONG-SAN" POTTERY POURING BOWL OF

HAKEME TYPE (YI DYNASTY)

Height, 3 1/2 in. Diameter, 9 3/16 in. Private Collection

In the foothills of Kyeryong-san, a famous mountain situated about twelve miles west of Taejon in South Chungcheong province, there was a kiln named Hakbong-ri, which produced a variety of fine pottery wares during the Yi period, including wares with Punch'ōng-type decoration, plain black pottery, plain white wares, and pottery decorated in black brushwork over a white slip in the manner of the bowl illustrated here.

This particular pouring vessel is very highly regarded in Japan for its artless charm, and particularly for the humorous simplicity of the brushwork designs of both the exterior and the interior.

142. SMALL CUP OF *KOHIKI* TYPE WITH PAINTED DECORATION

Height, 1 7/8 in. Diameter, 3 1/4 in. Private Collection

Pottery of the *kohiki* type with painted decoration is extremely rare. This little cup decorated in iron oxide with a very simple linear pattern is notable for its excellent workmanship and the sharpness of the potting. In some respects it resembles the *hakeme*-type pottery of Kyeryong-san (plate 141), but the grayish ferruginous body is of rather lighter weight, and it is thought to be a product of the Hambyong district in South Cholla province.

143. WINE CUP WITH *KOHIKI*-TYPE GLAZE

Height, 1 7/8 in. Diameter, 2 1/8 in. Private Collection

This lovable little cup is the same type of ware as the waterpot in plate 127. The Japanese nomenclature *kohiki* derives from the powdery appearance of the glaze. Most of the *kohiki* wares in Japan, which include tea bowls, wine bottles, and deep dishes, were brought from Korea several centuries ago and are thought to have been made early in the Yi dynasty at a number of different kilns in South Cholla province. In particular, the Hambyong district seems to have specialized in such pottery.

144. *IDO* TEA BOWL NAMED "MEISŌKYŪ"

Height, 4 1/8 in. Diameter, 5 7/8 in. Private Collection

Of all the tea-ceremony wares which reached Japan from Korea, those held in highest esteem are the so-called *Ido* tea bowls, of which the example illustrated here is considered one of the finest.

The favorites of tea-ceremony men during Kamakura and Muromachi times were the celadon and *temmoku* bowls of the Sung dynasty, but with the advent of the humanistic movement toward the end of the sixteenth century, and under the guidance of such famous tea masters as Jukō and Rikyū, preference was given to the products of Korean folk art and their Japanese counterparts, such as the wares of Shino, Hagi, Karatsu, and the Raku pottery. These wares appeal to the devotees of the tea ceremony because they are free from prescribed limitations of form and design, and are rich in a simple modest kind of beauty.

This *Ido* tea bowl, which belongs to the class known in Japan as *Meibutsu-de* (far-famed), has a body of coarse light-brown clay covered with a thick, apricot-yellow-stained, creamy glaze deeply crackled all over its surface. The form, with its deep body and tall foot in the bamboo-node shape, is impressively vigorous.

145. FOLK POTTERY JAR WITH IRON-BROWN DECORATION

Height, 11 ³/₈ in.   Diameter, 13 ⁷/₈ in.   Private Collection

Some of the folk art of the Yi period possesses a special charm and great humor. The rather crude but very animated tiger painted in underglaze iron-brown on this jar is an unfailing source of amusement and delight to the beholder. The jar itself, though slightly misshapen, is of nearly perfect proportions, and the simplicity of form and complete lack of artifice bear witness to the dexterity of hand and sureness of eye of the Korean potter who made it. It is difficult to date the pottery of the early and middle Yi period very precisely, but this piece probably dates from the fifteenth or early sixteenth century.

146. BLUE-AND-WHITE BOTTLE VASE

WITH DESIGN OF AUTUMN GRASSES (YI PERIOD)

Height, 9 5/16 in. Private Collection

This graceful bottle vase, which is one of the most delightful of known examples of early Korean blue-and-white porcelain, is of a type highly appreciated in Japan. The modesty and freedom of the form, the soft warm glaze, the utter simplicity of the decoration, and its quiet misty-blue color—all these features appeal strongly to Japanese connoisseurs, who pay large sums for such pieces.

According to the opinion of Dr. Asakawa, this vase may have been made at the official factory at Kwangju in Kyonggi-dō for presentation by the ruler to a senior official, probably some time in the sixteenth century—that is, during the early period of Yi dynasty blue-and-white wares.

147. BOTTLE VASE WITH *TESSHA* DECORATION (YI PERIOD)

Height, 11 3/4 in. Private Collection

Decorated wares of this kind, with the design applied in iron oxide under the glaze, are called by the Japanese *tessha*. Their charm lies in their crude but vigorous potting and the swiftly drawn, rather abstract patterns of the underglaze decoration.

The vase illustrated has a precisely executed, wildly abstract design like a sprig of plum blossom. On the reverse side is a single spray of bamboo leaves and the Chinese character for "wine." The body is a gray porcelaneous stoneware covered with transparent white glaze. Wares of this type with iron-oxide decoration under the glaze were made at a great many places all over North and South Korea during the Yi period, but the most famous centers of production were Kwangju and Koyong in Kyonggi province, Seongcheon in Pyongan, Mokcheon in South Chungcheong province, and Chungju and Koesan in North Chungcheong province.

This striking bottle vase, which dates from the middle of the Yi period, is most probably a product of the Mokcheon district.

CERAMICS OF ANNAM, THAILAND AND THE RYŪKYŪS

ANNAMESE CERAMICS

ANNAMESE ceramic history goes back further into antiquity than that of any other country in the Orient after China. During the T'ang dynasty, Annam was under the suzerainty of China, and in fact the name stems from the Chinese An-nan (Control over Southern Regions) Viceroyalty established north of Hanoi. The area was afterward called variously Cochin, Ou-ho, Nan-yüeh, Wan-ch'un, Ta-chü-yüeh, and Ta-nan.

Annamese ceramic art, like that of China, has a history of at least two thousand years. There are wares made in the manner of the Chinese wares of the Han and Six Dynasties periods; those imitating the T'ang and Sung wares, and later the Ming and Ch'ing; in short, the Annamese potters were at all times under Chinese influence. Annamese ceramics can be roughly classified into: (1) ancient earthenware prior to the eighth century; (2) wares from the ninth to the twelfth and thirteenth centuries, in which the influence of T'ang and Sung ceramics was paramount; (3) wares influenced by the blue-and-white and enameled porcelain of Yüan and Ming; and (4) wares made after the beginning of the seventeenth century.

1. In recent years the study of ancient Annamese ceramics has made good progress and by the efforts of French scholars of the Ecole Française d'Extrème Orient, as well as a number of Japanese scholars, in particular Messrs. Matsumoto, Yamamoto, and Kobayashi, it has been established that there were numerous tumuli of the Han to the T'ang and Sung periods in northern Annam, in the districts of Quang-yên, Bac-ninh, and Thanh-hoa. Objects excavated from these burial mounds comprise bronzes, coins, iron implements, jades, stone implements, glass articles, and others, including great quantities of ancient pottery. Among the ceramic objects excavated in the Tongking area the oldest seem to have been copied from old Chinese pottery; there is, for example, a considerable number of objects, including vases all but identical to Han bronze *tsun*, and models of towered pavilions and pig pens which are evidently copies of those frequently found among funerary ornaments of the Han period. The marked similarity of these objects to the Chinese wares in shapes and styles might lead one to imagine that they were brought from China, but Professor Janse has reported that at Dong-son in Thanh-hoa he discovered more than twenty kiln sites, datable to the Han period, where these pottery objects were evidently made.

After the glazed wares in sequence is a hard ware resembling the Japanese Sueki-type pottery, probably dating from between the third and sixth centuries, of which examples have been found in considerable numbers. It is a fairly high-fired pottery, and some pieces have a natural glaze running down to the shoulder. The Finot Museum in Hanoi possesses a wine pot made in imitation of a Chinese *t'ien-chi-hu*—a vessel with a chicken-head spout and two square ears on the shoulder, which is a shape frequently seen among Yüeh pieces of the Six Dynasties period (plate 17).

2. Objects datable between the seventh and the ninth century include jars, vases, and bowls apparently copied from T'ang Yüeh celadons and Kwangtung white porcelains.

Annamese ceramics of the tenth to the twelfth and thirteenth centuries show the strong influence of Chinese Sung ceramics. Bowls and dishes imitating the Northern celadons with incised decoration under an olive-green celadon glaze are typical of this period (plate 152). There are also many other pieces which appear to have been copied from Lung-ch'üan celadon, and although the color of these wares is not so beautiful as that of the Southern Sung celadons, the shapes and decorative styles are obviously inspired by the Chekiang group of celadons (plate 148).

White porcelains include copies of Northern Sung Ching-tê-chên ware popularly called *ying ch'ing*, and pieces which appear to be copies of Ting ware or perhaps the Ch'ao ware of Kwangtung (plate 153). There are also specimens in the style of Tz'ū Chou—pottery with designs of flowers, arabesque patterns, or figures painted in iron on a white ground. The main differences between these Annamese wares and the Chinese pottery of Hopei, Honan, and Shansi are that they are not coated with white slip, which is a characteristic of Tz'ū Chou-type wares, the paste is fine and smooth, and the subjects of the decoration are relatively rich in local color. Among other pottery resembling the Chinese Sung wares in shapes and styles, there is a plain dark-brown ware, a ware with black-brown glaze, and a ware covered all over with a fresh green glaze something like the Japanese green Oribe. These Sung-style Annamese ceramics are generally termed Thanh-hoa ware, presumably because the known examples came chiefly from tumuli in Thanh-hoa.

3. During the period from the fourteenth to the sixteenth century, blue-and-white and red-enameled wares were produced in Annam under the influence of Chinese blue-and-white and enameled wares of the Yüan and Ming periods. The most celebrated example of Annamese porcelain of this period is a blue-and-white vase with peony design in the Topkapu Sarayi Museum at Istanbul, which was described in detail by the English scholar Hobson in the *Transactions of the Oriental Ceramic Society, 1933–1934*. It is a large pear-shaped vase about two feet in height, with a beautiful dignified form, executed in an exceptionally elaborate style and design. In underglaze blue on the shoulder is an inscription reading "The year T'ai-ho 8 [1450]. Maker..." The ware is a fine grayish-white semiporcelain with an exposed base, which is washed with the reddish-brown glaze characteristic of Annamese ceramics. No

[348]

other dated specimens have been found, but blue-and-white and enameled pieces, which, judging from their style, date from about the fourteenth to the sixteenth century, were imported to Japan in fairly large numbers (plate 155). Most of these came from the East Indies, and only a small proportion was brought directly from Annam.

4. Among Annamese ceramics of the seventeenth century and after is a group comprising mostly tea bowls, pitchers, and vases known in Japan as *Annan Shibori-de* (Annamese "squeezed"-type, blue-and-white wares, on which the blue has run down in streaks) or *Annan Tombo-de* (Annamese "dragonfly"-type, blue-and-white, with irregular designs appearing more or less like dragonflies), which were taken to Japan in the late Momoyama to the early Edo periods and have ever since been prized for use in the tea ceremony (plate 149). A crude enameled ware, known in Japan as *beni* (pink) *Annan,* also began to be made early in the seventeenth century. In the late seventeenth to the eighteenth century, it appears that *wu-ts'ai* (five colors) and *fên ts'ai* (powder colors), imitating Ch'ing ceramics, were made in quantities in Annam. In short, Annamese ceramics were always under Chinese influence, and Annamese products of each period resembled their Chinese counterparts. However, although Annamese ceramics are inferior in technique and somewhat lacking in elegance and variety in comparison with the Chinese, they are not without charm and have a certain "dreamy" quality which appeals to Japanese connoisseurs.

THAI CERAMICS

It is not yet clearly known when pottery began to be made in Thailand, but it may be inferred that the development of ceramic art was much later than in China or Annam. One theory holds that pottery existed already in the sixth or seventh century, but another opinion is that it did not make its appearance until about the thirteenth century when there was a large-scale migration into this region. Whichever theory is correct, it was in the thirteenth to the fifteenth century that the well-known Sawankhalok ware, generally regarded as the most representative of Thai ceramics, was produced. Unfortunately, the manufacture of this unique Thai pottery continued for only a hundred to a hundred and fifty years.

The concept which has heretofore been held about Thai ceramics is derived from the theories of Mr. Miki, Mr. Saga, and Mr. Reginald le May (one of the outstanding authorities on Thai pottery and art) that pottery manufacture began after King Rāma Kamhêng—who is supposed to have visited China in 1294, and possibly again in 1300—brought back Chinese potters with him and built kilns at Sukhotai. The sites of these old kilns are said to be at Sukhotai, Sawankhalok, and Chieng Sen. Some recent writers, however, notably the late Mr. Phraya Nakorn Phrah Ram, have tried to upset this tradition. In his book *Tai Pottery,* Mr. Phraya Nakorn records the opinion that the origin of Thai ceramics is far earlier than believed heretofore, and that the manufacture of pottery began in fact in the sixth or seventh century. He divides the products of Sawankhalok, the site of the largest Thai ceramic center, into the C'alieng and Satc'analai periods and states that the Sawankhalok factory of the C'alieng period, the oldest of Thai ceramic kilns, was established in about 500 A.D., at approximately the same time as the establishment of the State of Sawankhalok, and lasted for 874 years until it was abandoned in 1374. He also advances the theory that in about 568 (or, according to another system of dating, in about 756), the year in which the State of Chieng Sen was established, a pottery factory was started at Kalong and continued active until the year 1359 when Th'ammarac'a II, the king of Sukhotai, invaded the area and carried off the Kalong potters to Sukhotai. There, under the patronage of the king, they built the first Sukhotai kilns; but as the territory of Th'ammarac'a II was conquered in 1374 by the king of Ayuthia, the factory lasted for only about fifteen years.

According to the same theory, the Sawankhalok kilns of the Satc'analai period were built close to those of the C'alieng period shortly after the latter were abandoned in 1374. In 1446 a turncoat governor named P'aya Yut'itsacieng, followed by the inhabitants of this area, moved to Chiêngmai, taking the Sawankhalok potters with him, and the kilns at Sawankhalok ceased to function from that time. The Sawankhalok kilns of the Satc'analai period, therefore, were active for only seventy-two years.

This theory of Mr. Phraya Nakorn admits of some doubt. In particular, the opinion that the C'alieng and Kalong factories were in existence as long ago as the sixth or seventh century lacks corroboration and cannot be seriously entertained.

The site of the Sawankhalok kilns of the C'alieng period is supposed to be located near the ruins of an old castle west of the present community of Sawankhalok across the river Chao Phraya, and the ware which Mr. Phraya Nakorn ascribes to the C'alieng period comprises not only pieces with transparent celadon glaze but also jars, bottles, covered boxes, and bowls, covered all over with a black-brown glaze; and bowls, covered boxes, and Buddhist statues, covered with an opaque white-ash glaze known in Japan as *shirahagi* glaze. It is very questionable, however, whether any of these dates back earlier than the thirteenth century.

The kiln sites of Kalong which were discovered in 1933 are situated about nine miles south of Wieng Papao, a community in the north of Thailand, approximately halfway between Chiêngmai and Chiêngrai. Ruins of several kilns along the Menam Lao, one of the branches of the Mekong River, have also been reported, and it is said that there are some kiln sites at Wieng Ho and Amp'ho Che situated about five miles from Wieng Papao. The shards found scattered on the Kalong sites are by and large similar in style, but are unlike any of the kinds previously known. The majority of them are pieces with iron painting on a Sawankhalok-style white ground, but the designs are different from those of either the Sawankhalok or the Sukhotai ware, and are more like the Chinese Tz'ū Chou ware. The Kalong kilns also seem to have produced plain bowls, boxes with covers, jars, and so on, covered with a finely crackled transparent white glaze faintly tinged with blue. Kalong pieces are, however, rarely to be seen in Japan.

The ruins of the Sukhotai kilns are situated about twenty miles west of the present town of Sukhotai with the Menam River between. Close by to the south is the site of the ruined Sukhotai castle. Briefly, Sukhotai ware does not include any celadon; the majority of known pieces have decoration in iron painting on a white ground in the manner of the Chinese Tz'ū Chou ware, and the ware differs from the Sawankhalok ware in that the body, which is of coarse clay, is coated with white slip. The predominant design is a single fish painted in the center medallion (plate 157), but there are some examples with designs of flowering plants or birds in flight.

The Sawankhalok kilns of the Satc'analai period appear to have been situated just north of the kilns of the C'alieng period. According to Mr. Phraya Nakorn, the Sawankhalok ware of the Satc'analai period included some plain specimens with black-brown glaze or transparent white glaze, but it was mostly of a type known in Japan as *Sunkoroku*, that is, with iron painting on a white ground. Products of the Sawankhalok kilns, which are the most numerous of surviving Thai pottery articles, comprise a rich variety of wares, which may be broadly grouped into the following four types:

1. *Celadon.* A ware made under the strong influence of Southern Sung Lung-ch'üan yao. It has a coarse, gray, semiporcelaneous body thickly covered with a crackled, transparent, and relatively pale celadon glaze (plate 158). The glaze is usually a greenish color tinged with blue, but occasionally it is a dull gray-blue or dark gray. Shallow bowls, about twelve inches in diameter, are a predominant shape, but there are also jars, bottles, globular vases with ears, boxes with covers, and wine cups. While Sawankhalok celadon has a strange, simple beauty, it cannot compare in quality with the celadons of Lung-ch'üan or even with many of the lesser export wares of the contemporary Chinese private kilns. It was often cracked or damaged in the firing, and there are frequently imperfections in the glaze. Moreover, the Sawankhalok potters used a long horizontal kind of kiln in which the heat was often unevenly distributed, and it is only too evident that some of these kilns were poorly constructed. They often collapsed during the firing, and their contents, being damaged beyond repair, were not removed until, in modern times, the collapsed kilns were excavated, revealing bent or twisted pots, or several vessels fused together by their molten glaze. There are also examples of kilns which were apparently abandoned before the pottery could be removed after firing, suggesting the hasty flight of the potters because of invasion or some other disaster.

2. *Black glaze.* Pottery with black or black-brown glaze was the most common and most widely made throughout the history of twenty centuries of Oriental ceramics, and it is still being turned out in large quantities at various places. In Thailand, according to Mr.

Phraya Nakorn, black-glazed wares were made at C'alieng, Kalong, Sukhotai, and Satc'analai. The bodies of these wares vary slightly but the glazes are very similar. Most of the black pottery wares of Thailand took the form of large pots or urns. In addition there are small jars, covered vessels, and bowls.

3. *White opaque glaze.* Thai wares with a white opaque glaze, known in Japan as *shira-hagi* glaze, are found in China, Korea, and Japan as well as in Thailand. Existing specimens of this type are not so numerous as celadons and white porcelains with iron-brown decoration. However, jars, vases, covered vessels, bowls, dishes, Buddhist statues, and the roof-ridge ornaments called *shiki* by the Japanese are sometimes to be seen.

4. *Iron painting on white ground.* The Thai pottery with iron painting on a white ground was made at Kalong, Sukhotai, and at Sawankhalok during the Satc'analai period. Pieces from Kalong are characterized by a relatively coarse decoration, and show the strong influence of the Chinese Tz'ū Chou yao. The wares made in Sukhotai have a body of coarse red clay washed with white slip, and many of the specimens are shallow bowls with simple ornaments—for example, a single fish or a single flowering branch—painted in the center medallion. Sawankhalok pieces are generally decorated with the elaborate arabesque designs peculiar to Thailand, and the body is a hard, gray, semiporcelaneous paste (plate 159). In terms of quantity, pieces from Sawankhalok are the most numerous; Sukhotai wares are seen much less frequently, while Kalong pieces are very rare. This type of pottery with iron painting on a white ground far outnumbers all other Thai ceramics, and in Japan it is this particular kind which is evoked by the term *Sukoroku*. Professor O. Beyer ascribes the ware to the fifteenth century, but Mr. Phraya Nakorn believes that some specimens date from the thirteenth or the fourteenth century.

In addition to all these, unglazed, high-fired pottery wares were produced at the kilns of C'alieng, Kalong, Sukhotai, and Satc'analai. Large waterpots of this type are in fact still made to this day in Bangkok, Chiêngmai, and Ubon. They are a gray ware, mostly plain but sometimes with engraved lines or applied ornaments. If the Sawankhalok and Kalong kilns have indeed existed since the fifth or sixth century, as Mr. Phraya Nakorn would have us believe, they must certainly have produced wares of this kind, but such wares, if they survive, are not identified.

CERAMICS OF THE RYUKYUS

Pottery production in the Ryūkyū Islands is traditionally believed to have originated with one Chō Kenkō (otherwise Ichiroku Reishin), a Korean potter naturalized in Japan, who went to the Ryūkyūs in 1682 from Naeshirogawa, in the province of Satsuma, at the invitation of Hisatoyo, heir to the king of the Ryūkyū Islands, with the consent of Yoshihisa Shimazu, Lord of Satsuma. There is reason to believe, however, that the true origin of Ryūkyū ceramics goes back to the Momoyama period or even earlier. Up to the present the sites of four principal centers of ceramic production have been discovered in the main island of Okinawa: Wakuta, at Kami Izumi-machi, Naha City; Takaraguchi, at Momohara-machi-machi, Shuri City; Chibana, at Misato-mura, Nakagami-gun; and Kogachi, at Haneji-mura, Kunigami-gun. Besides these, it seems that there was a factory on Yaeyama Island, established by one Karechigen Nakamura. This, however, was built probably in about the Kyōho era (1716–1735), and was active for only a short period.

Of the four ceramic centers in Okinawa Main Island, the one at Wakuta, which is supposed to have been the place where Chō Kenkō started his kiln, appears to have been most active. Shards found on a number of old kiln sites in this area are unglazed, highly ferrous, black-brown, coarse pottery of a type known in Japan as *Namban* (plate 160).

The site of the old Takaraguchi kilns is now a built-up area and the exact locations are not known, although they are referred to in old records. The remains of the Chibana kilns are situated at Misato-mura, a village in the middle of Okinawa where a number of shards, mostly of the *Namban* type, have been found scattered in a cultivated field about one hundred yards square. The *Kyuyō*, a historical document of the Ryūkyūs, states that the factories at Wakuta, Takaraguchi, and Chibana were abandoned in 1682, and that the ceramic industry previously active in these places was concentrated in an area near the modern town of Tsuboya in Naha.

The existence of kiln sites at Kogachi was not suspected until Mr. Eikichi Yamasato discovered them. He reports that shards of black-glazed pottery resembling Old Seto ware and of ash-glazed pottery are found on the site, but none of the *Namban* type. According to local tradition, the kilns here were abandoned during the reign of Kei-ō (1713–1752) owing to the forestry, conservation policy of the then Premier Sai On, but in the absence of any written record concerning these kilns it is not possible to reach a firm conclusion as to when they were active. Judging from the shards, however, the ware appears to date from about the eighteenth century.

After the kilns were concentrated at Tsuboya in 1682, they produced a ware known in the Ryūkyūs as *Jo-yaki* (quality ware), a glazed pottery with decoration in overglaze colors, or else with engraved designs or white slip painting. The *Namban* ware, called *So-yaki* (coarse ware), also continued to be made in quantity. Of the present-day kilns now active in the Ryūkyūs, the most numerous are those manufacturing *Namban* ware, which may fairly be considered the representative pottery of the Ryūkyūs.

148. DEEP BOWL OF ANNAMESE CELADON

WITH MOLDED DESIGN OF *SHINOGI* (RIDGES)

Height, 4 3/16 in. Diameter, 5 11/16 in. Private Collection

Three or four different kinds of celadon wares were made in Annam from the eighth or ninth century onward. This splendid deep bowl, which is perhaps a product of Dong-son in Thanh-hoa in the thirteenth century, is of a type commonly called Thanh-hoa ware. The body is a fine chalky-white clay covered with a semitransparent olive-colored glaze. The *Shinogi* design on the exterior is no doubt copied from the celadon wares of Lung-ch'üan, but the form and glaze color are more reminiscent of the Northern celadon wares of Ju Chou. The quiet modesty and pleasing freshness of this bowl make it one of the most memorable examples of Annamese pottery. It was taken to Japan by Mr. A. Nagata, who acquired it while he was serving as Japanese Consul-General at Hanoi.

149. ANNAMESE TEA BOWL

WITH BLUE UNDERGLAZE DECORATION OF DRAGONFLIES

Height, 3 5/16 in.   Diameter, 4 13/16 in.   Private Collection

Tea bowls of this type, with blue decoration under a low-fired glaze, were taken to
Japan toward the end of the sixteenth or early in the seventeenth century and
ever since have been highly prized for use in the tea ceremony. The blue painting
is always blurred and indistinct, and the subjects include bird and flower designs,
lotus-flower arabesques, human figures, birds in flight, and small boats, but the
best known and most highly regarded are those with a design of dragonflies like
the bowl illustrated. Most of the known examples have an exposed foot washed
with a reddish-brown glaze, but in some of the finer-quality pieces the foot is
covered with white glaze.

Wares of this type were made in the general area of Bat-trang in the north
of Annam as well as a number of other places, but more precise identification of
the places of manufacture must await further research.

150. ANNAMESE TEA BOWL

WITH DECORATION IN OVERGLAZE ENAMELS

Height, 4 5/8 in. Diameter, 4 1/4 in. Tokugawa Museum, Nagoya

Colored Annamese tea bowls of this type, known in Japan as *beni Annan,* or pink
Annam ware, are even rarer than the blue-and-white bowls described in the notes
to plate 149; in fact, apart from this example, which has been in Japan since the
end of the sixteenth century, the only other one known is a similar bowl now in
the Tokyo National Museum which was taken to Japan from Java a few years
ago. The body and shape are in every way similar to the blue-and-white wares,
but the design of chrysanthemums and intertwined stems is applied over the glaze
in red and green enamels. Pottery decorated in this manner in the shapes of deep
bowls, dishes, and saucers has been recovered in relatively large quantities from
a number of places in the East Indies, and it is thought that it was made for export
in northern Annam during the fifteenth and sixteenth centuries.

151. SAWANKHALOK SHALLOW BOWL

Height, 3 1/16 in.   Diameter, 8 1/4 in.   Private Collection

This bowl of Sawankhalok pottery looks at first glance like a piece of blue-and-white ware, but in fact it is decorated with iron oxide applied under a semi-transparent bluish glaze. The simple but graceful design of floral sprays surrounding the outside of the bowl lends it an air of quiet distinction. Sawankhalok ware of this kind, which was made in Thailand during the fourteenth or fifteenth century, appears to have been exported in large quantities to the neighboring countries of Southeast Asia and particularly to Java and the Celebes. This piece was taken to Japan from the East Indies in recent years.

152. ANNAMESE CELADON SHALLOW BOWL

WITH ENGRAVED DECORATION OF FLORAL SCROLLS

Height, 2 11/16 in. Dianeter, 7 in. Private Collection

This celadon bowl is very much like the Chinese so-called Northern celadon wares of Ju Chou with respect to both the shape and the olive-green color of the celadon glaze. The body, however, which is of a close-grained grayish earthenware, lacks the weight and "feel" of the Chinese ware.

The inside of the bowl is decorated with a simple band of floral scrolls incised in the body under the glaze in the manner of the Sung wares of North China; the exterior is plain. There are five small spur marks on the interior glaze surface, implying that the bowl was fired with several others, each piled on top of another.

153. ANNAMESE WHITE PORCELAIN SAUCER DISH

WITH ENGRAVED DECORATION OF PEONY SCROLLS

Height, 1 13/16 in. Diameter, 6 5/8 in. Private Collection

This saucer dish of a type commonly called Thanh-hoa pottery is somewhat reminiscent of the Sung Ting yao, although it is yellowish in color rather than white and the glaze has a fine crackle or crazing all over the surface, unlike Ting ware, which is never crackled. The body is a smooth, grayish, porcelaneous ware covered with a clear glaze tinged with yellow, and the decoration of peony scrolls is engraved in relief beneath the glaze in the manner of Ting yao. The exterior is plain and the foot is exposed. Five small spurmarks on the inside of the dish indicate that it was fired with others piled up on top of it in the same way as the celadon bowl of plate 152.

154. ANNAMESE WHITE DISH WITH INCISED DECORATION

Height, 2 13/16 in. Diameter, 14 3/16 in. National Museum, Tokyo

This large dish, which was taken to Japan from Java a few years ago, is made in the style of Chinese wares of the early Ming period. It is remarkable for the technique of its decoration, which is engraved under the glaze in a manner known in China as "concealed decoration." The body is an almost pure white, hard-fired stoneware covered with a semiopaque milk-white glaze without crackle. In the center of the dish, incised into the body by line engraving with a sharp tool, is a landscape scene surrounded by a double circle and a band of floral scrolls. The outside of the dish is also similarly decorated with a simple line engraving of a floral pattern, and the foot, which is exposed, is covered with a thin wash.

"Concealed decoration" of this kind is occasionally seen on white porcelain wares of the Hsüan Tê period of the Ming dynasty, and this rare dish was no doubt inspired by such a piece, but no other example is known among existing Annamese wares.

155. ANNAMESE BLUE-AND-WHITE SHALLOW DISH

WITH DESIGN OF BIRDS IN FLIGHT AMONG GRASSES

Diameter, 10 5/8 in. National Museum, Tokyo

This is an Annamese blue-and-white dish of the fifteenth century in which the influence of early Ming blue-and-white is clearly recognizable. The body is a close-grained, grayish, porcelaneous ware covered with a transparent white glaze without crackle. The design of two birds in flight among grasses, surrounded by stylized floral sprays, is painted in a blackish gray-blue color under the glaze. The exterior is similarly decorated with simple floral sprays, and the foot, which is exposed, is covered with a thin wash of transparent glaze. Other dishes of this kind are known which have designs of fish, birds, flowers, and animals, all betraying the influence of early Ming blue-and-white porcelain. The precise locality of Annam in which these wares were made during the fifteenth or early sixteenth century is not yet determined, but it may have been in the vicinity of Bat-trang near Hanoi.

156. ANNAMESE BLUE-AND-WHITE TALL INCENSE BURNER

WITH DECORATION OF DRAGON AND CLOUDS

Height, 27 9/16 in. Diameter, 10 7/8 in. Tokugawa Museum, Nagoya

This very remarkable piece of Annamese blue-and-white ware in the form of a tall stand surmounted by an incense burner was taken to Japan at the end of the sixteenth century or early in the seventeenth century, and shortly afterward came into the possession of the Tokugawa family. The body is a close-grained grayish porcelaneous ware covered with a crackled, transparent, white glaze. A magnificent dragon, precisely modeled in relief, curls around the jar, and the cloud decoration is painted under the glaze in the splotchy blue characteristic of Annamese blue-and-white pottery. The incense burner itself is decorated with six ornamental rosettes and has four feet sculptured in the form of lion heads.

[369]

157. SUKHOTAI SHALLOW DISH WITH FISH DECORATION

Height, 2 1/4 in.   Diameter, 7 7/8 in.   Private Collection

Sukhotai wares decorated with a single fish motif are by no means rare, but the quality of the painting on this dish is unusually good.

The body is a coarse reddish earthenware with a coating of white slip. The fish design is painted on this base in iron oxide, and the whole is covered with a clear white glaze.   The exterior of the dish is undecorated and the foot is exposed. According to local tradition, the Sukhotai wares date from the year 1294, when the Thai king returned from a visit to China bringing with him potters from Tz'ū Chou who established kilns at Sukhotai under the king's patronage. However, within a space of fifteen years the kilns were closed down and rebuilt in the vicinity of Sawankhalok. The technique of decorating in iron-brown over a white slip seen on this dish is clearly recognizable as a continuation of the Tz'ū Chou tradition.

The Sukhotai wares seem to have been exported in large quantities to the neighboring countries of Southeast Asia and particularly to the East Indies. This piece was taken to Japan in recent years from Java.

158. SAWANKHALOK DEEP DISH WITH CELADON GLAZE

Height, 3 9/16 in. Diameter, 10 5/8 in. Private Collection

Most of the surviving examples of Sawankhalok celadon ware in Japan were excavated from sites in the East Indies—particularly Java and Celebes, which were evidently important export markets for Thai pottery in the fourteenth to the sixteenth centuries. The ware has a hard-fired semiporcelaneous body, covered with a soft, bluish-green, crackled celadon glaze. This deep dish, which was taken to Japan from the East Indies in recent years, has a simple decoration of stylized flowers and leaves broadly engraved under the glaze. The exterior is undecorated and the foot is exposed. It is considered to have been made at Sawankhalok, probably in the early fourteenth century.

159. FOUR SAWANKHALOK COVERED BOXES

Heights: upper right, 3 $^7/_{16}$ in.; lower right, 3 $^{11}/_{16}$ in.;

upper left, 2 $^{15}/_{16}$ in.; lower left, 3 $^7/_8$ in. Private Collection

Sawankhalok covered boxes of this type, which are too large for use in the tea ceremony as incense boxes and too small to be used as food containers, seem to have reached Japan in relatively large numbers, some from the ruins of kiln sites in Thailand, but mostly from excavations in the East Indies. They were apparently made at Sawankhalok for export during the fourteenth and fifteenth centuries, and the four examples illustrated here give some idea of the wealth of different forms and designs in which the Sawankhalok wares of the time were made. In every case, the body is a grayish-white semiporcelaneous clay. The one at the upper right, which is covered with an opaque white glaze, has a lid engraved with a simple design of arabesques under a thin toffee-colored glaze. The one on the lower right has the usual sort of Sawankhalok underglaze decoration in iron oxide, but, additionally, both box and cover are molded with twelve panels.

The two on the left are both engraved with a design of arabesques which is covered with a thin toffee-colored glaze, leaving the grayish body exposed.

Each of the four pieces has a low unglazed foot.

160. *NAMBAN* WATERPOT FROM THE RYŪKYŪS

Height, 5 1/2 in. Diameter 10 in. Private Collection

This is a fine massive *Namban* waterpot of a type which has long commanded the admiration of tea-ceremony people, who find in such wares a most satisfying rustic charm. It is a coarse, ferruginous, unglazed earthenware fired at a relatively high temperature.

The dating of these Ryūkyū wares is very difficult, owing to lack of reliable data about the kilns which produced them, but this example is tentatively placed in the middle of the Edo period—that is to say, about the middle of the eighteenth century.

A SHORT BIBLIOGRAPHY

IN ENGLISH

BUSHELL, S.W. *Description of Chinese Pottery and Porcelain, Being a Translation of the T'ao Shuo.* Oxford, 1910.

GRAY, BASIL. *Early Chinese Pottery and Porcelain.* London, 1953.

HOBSON, R.L. *Chinese Pottery and Porcelain.* 2 vols. London, 1915.

HONEY, W.B. *The Ceramic Art of China and Other Countries of the Far East.* London, 1945.

SAYER, G.R. *Ching-tê-Chên T'ao Lu,* or the Potteries of China. London, 1949.

The Chinese Exhibition: A Commemorative Catalogue of the International Exhibition of Chinese Art, Royal Academy of Arts, November, 1935–March 1936. London, 1936.

Transactions of the Oriental Ceramic Society, London. From 1921.

Far Eastern Ceramic Bulletin. From 1948.

Oriental Art. From 1948.

MITSUOKA, TADANARI. *The Ceramic Art of Japan* (Tourist Library Vol. 8). Japan Travel Bureau, Tokyo, 1949.

IN JAPANESE

KOYAMA, FUJIO. *Shina Seiji Shi-ko* (A History of Chinese Celadon). Tokyo, 1943.

Tōji (Oriental Ceramics). 1927–43.

Tōsetsu (Journal of the Japan Ceramic Society). From 1953.

Chugoku Meitō Hyaku-sen (One Hundred Selected Masterpieces of Chinese Ceramics). Edited by Fujio Koyama. Nihon Keizai Shimbun-sha, Tokyo, 1960.

IMAIZUMI, YUSAKA. *Nihon Tōji Shi* (History of Japanese Ceramics). Yuzankaku, Tokyo, 1925.

Ko-Imari. Ko-Imari Chōsa Iinkai (Committee for the Study of Old Imari). Kinkadō, Saga, 1959.

KOYAMA, FUJIO. *Nihon Bijutsu Taikei-Tōgei-hen* (General History of Japanese Art-Ceramics). Kōdansha, Tokyo, 1960.

KOYAMA, FUJIO. *Shōsōin Sansai* (Shōsōin Three-Color Ware). Zayuhō, Tokyo, 1947.

KOYAMA, FUJJO. *Tōyō Kotōji* (The Ancient Ceramics of the East). Vols. 1–7. Bijutsu Shuppansha, Tokyo, 1958. (The text of the present book is largely based on this work).

NABESHIMA, CHOKUSHŌ. *Kakiemon.* Kenkadō, Saga City, 1957.

Nippon no Tōji (The Ceramics of Japan). Edited by Seiichi Okuda and others. Tōto Bunka, Tokyo, 1954.

Sekai Tōji Zenshü (Compilation of Ceramics of the World). Vols. 1–16. Kawade Shōbo, Tokyo, 1955.

Tōki Daijiten (Ceramic Dictionary). Vols. 1–6. Edited by Kenichirō Hōunsha Ono. Tokyo 1937.

Tōki Zenshu (The Ceramic Series). Vols. 1–18. Edited by Fujio Koyama. Tokyo 1959.

IN CHINESE

CHEN, WAN-LI. *Chung Kuo Ch'ing Tz'u Shih Lue* (History of Chinese Celadon). Peking, 1956.

Wen Wu T'san K'ao Tzu Liao (Journal of Museums and Relics). Peking, 1954–58.